THE SAINT PLAYS

PAJ BOOKS

BONNIE MARRANCA
GAUTAM DASGUPTA
SERIES EDITORS

THE SAINT PLAYS

ERIK EHN

A PAJ BOOK

THE JOHNS HOPKINS UNIVERSITY PRESS
BALTIMORE AND LONDON

© 2000 Erik Ehn
All rights reserved. Published 2000
Printed in the United States of America on acid-free paper
9 8 7 6 5 4 3 2 1

The Johns Hopkins University Press
2715 North Charles Street
Baltimore, MD 21218-4363
www.press.jhu.edu

Library of Congress Cataloging-in-publication Data will
be found at the end of this book.
A catalog record for this book is available from the
British Library.

ISBN 0-8018-6287-6 (pbk.)

FOR PAT CHANTELOUBE-EHN

CONTENTS

PREFACE

These plays are some of many short pieces from an ongoing series on the lives of Catholic saints. The subject matter is exploded biography, or the means by which the self is overmastered by acts of the imagination, by acts of faith. The landscape is Christian according to the accident of my spiritual education, but the plays are religious chiefly in the sense that they look at individuals as inappropriately cast in division. Christianity is explored for its ways of believing and the patterns of its mysticism, abstracted to an esthetic physics.

Imagination, identified with faith and subject to moral proofs, is more than make-believe. The truth and fiction in the lives as they come to us work a blur (or hyperinvolved pattern) and stir up practical confusion. Figures slip death to be always becoming; we are invited to project ourselves into their metahistorical uproar, their irresolvable complexity, their constant approach. We are all charged with the task of turning into saints ourselves, with a responsibility to lose location and enter into a love so radical that identity surrenders to the condition of metaphor. To live in poetic oscillation with God is to live a poetry free of poetry or drama free of drama (metaphor is the space between resonating strings).

The Saint Plays is naturally an array of texts. There are more saints (ten thousand plus) than I can ever pull to paper. There is no way for the plays that have made it to the page to be produced in a complete or consistent way, because the set of them is definitionally incomplete and inconsistent. The series offers a polemic against the creation of objects (idolatry); narrative closure is idolatrous. The idea of an ending is in line with the notion that the individual is the primary unit of meaning in the social sentence, that classics (canonical, terminally fine reifications of theoretical principles) and the critics who make them are above and immune to the aniconic perpetual mess of the creative writing process, and that history, the evidence of the senses, science and reason control the poetics of truth. There is no synthetic ending overall, or generally, per play. Texts move forward in time but out from under the myth of rising action. All action is risen and unravels into exhaustion, drowning, decay, or bliss.

A saint is a human mandala — a life in a ritual shape held up as a focus for contemplation. The symbolic and literal are conflated to produce what Lorca calls the *hecho poetico* — the poetic fact — an irreducible image that is a source of meaning rather than a restatement of it. Saints make autobiography of conundrum, and practice right conduct on a field occupied simultaneously by the impossible and the ethical (by that which cannot be comprehended yet compels choice). Since saints act according to their faith and are defined by their actions, they live again in the faith of others, where faith is reenactment; they work themselves out through our prayer, through our reading (heaven isn't magic, it is reading). These sacred agents never mean or conclude, but they consume meaning as they move, taking up detail (acta) as fuel. They move not so as to be endless (extensive through time) but with intensity, to become instant, infinitely attractive, anomalous in time. And so the plays are short. They want to be over before they start.

Big Cheap Theater is the name of the esthetic. "Big" is past reach of discourse; cannot be reified; unstoppable. "Cheap" is common, public, complicit (St. Gertrude: "Property, the more common it is, the more holy it is"). "Theater" is hospitality — a living act of corporal mercy: text cares for an actor's body, and a production commits itself to the audience's body in a nursed space. (Hospitality is the *empty* bed; theater is not the bed but the inviting emptiness; theater gets itself out of the way as quickly as possible). Therefore the plays are gestural, close to the actor's body. The language aspires to breath-gesture. Language wants to be spectacle, hypnotic trigger. In practical terms, what the language does and how it does it (how it is breathed or sung) is more important than what it says. In terms of set, the radiantly compassionate flesh and blood performer *is* the elemental theater.

Wholly Joan's came first; *The Imp of Simplicity* is the latest; Edith Stein is likely next; there are many, many versions of Mary to do (the Version Mary). Each piece contains a pattern, a saint and a prayer. The pattern can be musical, mathematical, rhetorical; it can be invented, adapted, or stripped and reinvested (Eulalia's scene titles are taken from Lorca's poem on her martyrdom; *Tree of Hope* is built on a list of works Frida Khalo made for an exhibition; *The Imp* follows a series of quotations taken in order from *The Imitation of Christ*); there are patterns within patterns (rhyme, gesture). The saints are the fountainheads of imagery and of that difficulty that concentrates the imagination (Barbara and her volts; Kolbe's empathy). The prayer is that which God and the saint are not — the distance and its potential. The passionate gap is represented on time's map (when characters reach to each other across eras) or, again, on rhetoric's landscape (when difference is a question of language and tone). The pattern, the saint, and the prayer trip each other up (up and forward), hopefully break one another, hopefully advertise rest.

The Saint Plays are as broke, broken, broken down, and broken through as I can make them. The theology: Big Cheap Mysticism — here are little and poor vanishing acts.

THE SAINT PLAYS

WHOLLY JOAN'S

(Joan of Arc)

Characters

JOAN

GUARDS

ANGEL

Wholly Joan's was first presented at the Manhattan Class Company on September 8, 1988, directed by the playwright. Artistic directors: Bernard Telsey, Robert Lupone. Cast: Meg Anderson, Ken Adams, Christopher Randolph, Bernard Telsey, Kay Kowanko, Chaka, Cheri. Stage Manager: Mark Haverly.

Scene One: The Capture

(The stage is dark, but we hear JOAN's *steady tread. Then: a mouse-like shuffle; unseen guards move in. A circle of light falls like plate steel;* JOAN *delivers and retrieves weight, resisting the circle's physical pull.)*

JOAN   Not today. I don't think today. I don't know about this sometimes.

FIRST GUARD *(In a whisper, to the* SECOND*)*   I know where Joan of Arc is.

JOAN *(She doesn't hear them; still to the light.)*   Every time I do, something bad happens. No voices today.

FIRST GUARD   I know where to find Joan of Arc.

JOAN   You want me to love to hear you, but you can't make me.

FIRST GUARD   She always shows herself down here, around this time. She can't help herself.

JOAN   I know what it feels like. Don't rub it in. I know my skin gets warm and my eyes open. My joints get flexible. My hands get smart. I know what it feels like to be in the dead center with you. Not in the center of anything else — just pure center. The only thing. I know what it is to know a lot. That full feeling of a destiny I get after having eaten a restaurant breakfast with rough toast and coffee, working it all out on the back of a napkin with dad and all my sergeants. I remember what it is to be smart. *(Pause)* But I know that the center is a target. So don't try and change the subject.

FIRST GUARD   I hear something. Over there.

JOAN   If I could throw myself out to you, your voice — If I could throw myself away in your voice, without being caught . . . If you worked with guarantees . . .

FIRST GUARD   Right there.

JOAN   Then it wouldn't be work at all, and I'd get no wage. Okay. My God, I'm a lover. Jesus, I love you. Holy Ghost, I can't resist. *(She collapses into the light — she's young; she wears the coarse underclothes of a foot soldier and trails gleaming armor in her hands. An* ANGEL *appears. The* ANGEL *is three women. The first woman is the body of the* ANGEL, *the second the wings, the third and tallest holds her hands forward in an "o" for the halo. The actresses wear the nicest white dresses they own. They walk towards* JOAN *in unison; we are not certain whether they mean to help or hurt* JOAN.*)*

ANGEL *(Repeating, singing)*   Send my roots rain. *(They stop by* JOAN's *head and speak into her ear.)* Jumpin Jesus says to fight.

JOAN *(Up to the* ANGEL*)*   I hear every word. *(The* ANGEL *hurries off. Red police lights flash. Strong arms reach into the light and drag* JOAN *away.)*

Scene Two: The Defense

*(*JOAN *in a jail cell, manacled. She paces, laboriously, under the watch of the two* GUARDS. *A crowd outside calls for* JOAN's *release.)*

FIRST GUARD   Shut them up.

SECOND GUARD   I can't concentrate.

JOAN   It's overrated.

FIRST GUARD   Love everything you're ever going to love all of a sudden, honey, because you've come to the end of the line.

JOAN   That's the old line.

SECOND GUARD   We got to concentrate on how to get you out of here — out of our politics. Shut them the hell up. (JOAN *stops the chanting by astonishingly simple means.*)

JOAN   Tell everybody I'm a witch. You got reason to kill a witch.

FIRST GUARD   Far as I'm concerned, you're a kid sister who broke into the liquor cabinet and popped the emergency brake. We're killing you because you're a nuisance, and because we feel like it, and because daddy always liked us better. It just can't look that way.

JOAN   You're killing me because something loves me more than you know how. I got a lover with a cleaner eye and a longer stride than all your tech can crank.

SECOND GUARD   She's got a point, about the witchcraft. If we don't need a reason, we at least need an excuse.

FIRST GUARD   Who'll believe it? That she's a witch? (JOAN *lifts her bound hands, and the chains pop off. The* ANGEL *appears, with swords for her selves and a sword for* JOAN. *The* ANGEL *and* JOAN *do a dance that shows them fighting and overmastering the* GUARDS.)

JOAN   Think about the Columbia River. Think of all the steam buried in Wyoming. Think of all those distant natural mysteries you're afraid of. (*She knocks the* GUARDS *down, and trades the point of the sword between their two necks.*) I want you to try and stop me. I'm on a tear. I want you to dam me up. To try and cap me. Want my electricity released. Try and stop me, and I'll become the most powerful woman on the face of the earth.

FIRST GUARD   We will burn you.

SECOND GUARD   At the stake.

FIRST GUARD   To the ground.

Scene Three: The Burning

(JOAN *stands in tension, wearing full armor, in a volume of severe light. She's tied to a stake, and is on fire.*)

JOAN *(To God)*   You don't look away when I look at you. You don't stop when I refuse you. You don't refuse me. You are always moving towards me, and are moving me towards you, and you are always clear light, with the feel of cool water. As fierce as any burning gets, you are always cool and moving. Happy Valentine's day, God Almighty. You get my heart. I have nothing — no troops, no luck. Nothing to give you but a heart that listens. No love is stronger. No heart more abandoned. *(Her smiling face holds its expression as her head tips to one side. The light switches grips and discovers a large cloth heart downstage, flat and cherry red. The* GUARDS *enter and whisper.)*

FIRST GUARD   Her heart wouldn't burn. The body's gone — the heart's still here. Why wouldn't her heart burn with the rest of her body? *(The* SECOND GUARD *reaches into the light and touches the heart with his fingertips. Red hot. He retreats.)*

SECOND GUARD   BECAUSE HER HEART IS HOTTER THAN THE FIRE.

DASHBOARD

(Christopher)

Characters

AGATHA

EARLE

DAD

SOPHIA LOREN

Dashboard was first performed at the Annex Theatre in Seattle in April 1994, directed by the playwright. Artistic Director: Allison Narver. Cast: Robin Dicker, Hunt Holman, Josh Parks, Audrey Freudenberg. Ensemble: Kathleen Clarke, Audrey Freudenberg, Jody Hahn, John Holyoke, Heather Hughes, Natache LaFerriere. Band: Colin Stout, Heather Lewis, Michael Chick, Christina Mastin, Michael Shapiro. Production: James Keene, Ken Judy, Jonathan P. Walker, Julie Vadnais, Carlos Trevino, Maxmilian Bocek, Karl Gajdusek, Donald Crane, Tom Milewski, Andrew Lieberman, Heather Lewis, Suzanne Bybee, Gregory Musick, Margaret Doherty, Nancy Snapp, Kevin Mesher.

Scene One

(Italian film stars, Italian film music. Flash pictures all around. SOPHIA LOREN, *wearing long black silk gloves, steps onto a red carpet, walks up to a mahogany stand, and leans into a microphone.)*

SOPHIA   No pictures, no pictures. *(Blackout)*

Scene Two

(Center stage, a life-sized version of a dashboard Christopher glows in the dark. Christopher carries the boy Jesus on his shoulder; Christopher uses a staff. Stage right, a father drives with his twelve-year-old daughter down night's channel, wheat on either side of the car. Stage left, a gangly sixteen-year-old boy wearing blue jeans and a gray tee shirt sits on a book covered desk. The boy plays incredible guitar.)

DAD   Better than Brooklyn.

AGATHA   I don't think so.

DAD   Better than anyplace that's not Brooklyn out there.

AGATHA *(Eyes on the landscape)*   What's all this?

DAD   This is wheat.

EARLE   Gotta have a name. Got to. Beothormon. Whacamoginogen. Moby Dick. O . . . O . . . Offero.

DAD   A quiz.

AGATHA   What's the capital of Bored?

DAD   No. Say the name of the place.

AGATHA   Sapulpa, Oklahoma.

DAD   Sapulpa. Town stocks all the leading brands.

EARLE   Got to have a name.

AGATHA   They don't have Earle.

DAD   He'll be fine. We'll be fine.

AGATHA   You tired? You want me to drive?

DAD   No.

AGATHA   He's looking for a name. He needs me to help him with a confirmation name.

DAD   He's got a name.

AGATHA   Tomorrow is his confirmation.

DAD   Oh. That's in the present. We're here. You'll like it here.

AGATHA *(Indicating dash)*   Who's this?

DAD   He can't take this name.

AGATHA   Who is it?

DAD   Saint Christopher. They de-sainted him. Earle can take Christopher, but not this one.

AGATHA   Why do you keep it there?

DAD   Habit. I'm a creature of habit. Haven't had one for a while. Bought it special for the trip.

AGATHA   I've seen these.

DAD   He was a big one. The Italian movie stars put on a big protest outside the Vatican when it happened. Sophia Loren was there. You would have liked it. You and Earle. *(AGATHA sees EARLE.)*

AGATHA   And in an instant and in memory of me he's the Christopher himself.

EARLE   Offero. Yes. The freak.

DAD   Christ-bearer. Yes. That's his name. His name was Offero first, and he was a giant.

EARLE   Enduring this body, this sixteenth year, these hands/can't play.

AGATHA   Little deer-headed interloper, face jammed down the coal chute . . .

DAD   Sure, put whatever you want on the radio.

AGATHA   A time when I was eleven, Earle, we were there. My long, carved deer mask face at the coal chute of the house in Brooklyn. At the metalhead feast. Boy leader after the raid overseeing the hero's apportioning. *(She's up in the air with a deer mask on her face.)*

EARLE   I want to serve the greatest king. I want to liberate my sister from the tree.

DAD   He asked a monk who said: "Greatest service, lowest station." Just like you have there — the lowest station on the dial. Metal rules, huh?

AGATHA   Armor against death, Dad.

EARLE *(Rallying troops; music, nonstop)*   The objective is to accumulate the maximum sanctity and to pierce the wall between life and death, to make sure my sister is at peace. I read it can be done in the book *Gossamer Axe* by Gael Baudino.

DAD   I'll pull in here. One for the road, sweet daughter, I pray.

AGATHA   I'll stay out here.

DAD   Chris'll keep you company. Earle can choose that name, but not if it's that saint he means. They won't let him. *(He leaves.)*

EARLE   Any kind of sign or symbol or image you know.

AGATHA *(Climbing down)*   He was the ferryman. Walking people across the ford, so great big. Knew every rock.

EARLE   I'll go with the mighty oaf, Christopher. Take it in confirmation tomorrow. To liberate my sister from the tree. She got me started on this. I didn't have anything going, but she saw some guys in a restaurant playing "Besame Mucho" on big Mexican guitars, when Dad was a management consultant at Penny's in Albuquerque. Made Dad buy her one. At that point, she couldn't even hold it — it took the both of us. I'd be left hand, she's be right. And that was that. *(She is back to back with* EARLE. *She slips her arms through two loops, cruciform.* EARLE *walks.)*

AGATHA   Christopher lifted a child one day from the shoulder of the shore to his own shoulder.

EARLE   Power mad Saint Christopher on I-95. Gonna disimur my sister. Bring her back alive.

DAD *(Returning)*   Okay, let's go, Agatha. *(Drives)*

AGATHA   As he walked out into the river, the child grew heavier. Christopher thought he would drown.

EARLE *(The song is the journey through the water.)*
    Power mad Saint Christopher
    On I-95
    Gonna disimur my sister
    Gonna bring her back alive

    The brutal freak Saint Christopher
    Hyper-head churning wild

The buckling giant calls on almighty
Boy-Jesus hermaphrodite child

Christopher is drowning under
Neath the baby boy
The child is smiling patiently
Waiting out the ploy

They reach the western bank and
Christopher plants his staff
The staff breaks into flower
And the passenger has to laugh

What teeth hold the body
Is that a dream?
Is that a dream too?

I lost someone in the river
I lost my sister
I lost you

Boy-Jesus hermaphrodite ruler
Points with one hand to the tree
And there my sister hangs in peace
Drowned and waiting just for me

DAD   I don't believe in Christopher.

EARLE   Playing Spanish guitar and eating Italian food in a Swedish
town in Minnesota, waiting for our father to drive back from Brooklyn
with a scouting report, my sister Agatha discovered the station that gave
us the key to the land of the dead, into which we reached to stroke and
soothe the faces of our mother and many famous and glamorous people.

AGATHA   Dad Mom Earle Agatha in Albuquerque. Dad Mom Earle
Agatha in Jonesboro, Arkansas. Dad Earle Agatha in Raleigh, North
Carolina; in Riggins, Idaho; in Thief River, Minnesota; Brooklyn, New
York. Then Dad and Agatha down to Oklahoma. Dad ante's up Earle,
pitches him to Aunt Jack in New Rochelle for leaner life all new revue
down south. But children are strings shaken in a chord.

EARLE   When we found that station, that's when my sister and I developed infallible faith.

DAD   We must be across the border. Narcotic, Oklahoma. Injecting the white rabies of highway lines in through the third eye, inducing a right-hand downturn in the two-beer, hundred-mile-an-hour father. (EARLE goes to his knees. AGATHA *dismounts, and climbs a tree, deer mask visored back down.)*

AGATHA   The tire slips the lip, bursts and slurps off. The car spins at the rate of a sweep second hand into red rock. Agatha and her father erupt through the windshield like trout through water tension. (DAD *takes on his death.)* The fins of the old-style car shear off and lance the victims. Dad's caught in the jaws of the red rock, Modigliani head between falling rock molars. Agatha in a crab apple tree. When they find me, they think I am a road kill deer.

EARLE   The objective is to see her as she died, and not be afraid. To be fearless and past living. I believe in Saint Christopher, I don't care what anybody says. I will play any hard symbols I know through fusion stop-time to see my sister's cold face again. Christ equals the girl in the tree, and I can take it.

EARLE, AGATHA
    To pass through the water into death's air
    With music, is to pass through music

    To die without music, movies, mayhem
    Is to die without reason
    Is to die less than human

(The Italian film stars enter; they feed and clean the dead.) And the Italian film stars feed bread and wine — good bread, good wine — to the dead in the trees, in the rocks. Confirmation name: I take the banished name, for my sister.

16670

(Maxmilian Mary Kolbe)

Characters

KOLBE

GAJOWNICZEK

ZYMUNT

MARY

ANGELS

FACILITATOR (the FACILITATOR speaks some of the
stage directions and controls the mise en scène)

16670 first played at Intersection for the Arts in San Francisco in April
1993, directed by the playwright. Artistic director and producer: Paul
Codiga. Cast: Troy Anthony Harris, Robert Molossi, David Todd, Sam-
mie Choy, Jennifer Bainbridge, Denise Cavaliere, Johnna Marie Schmidt.
Production: Douglas Holmes, Colin Hale, Brook Stanton, Nina Siegal.
Live Music: Edith Rules (Derek Cheever, Leslie Jackson, Alan Whitman).

Scene One: Accounting

(An alarm clock rings and ZYMUNT *sits up in bed. He stops the alarm.)*

ZYMUNT   Nope. Not my play. *(Elsewhere,* GAJOWNICZEK *appears, in pajamas?)*

GAJOWNICZEK   But the moon was shone by one angel and the light was conveyed by another.

ZYMUNT   Let me sleep. *(Two* ANGELS *appear behind him. They have tattooed tears. One reveals the light of the moon, and the other presents the light to him.)*

GAJOWNICZEK   And there was no sleep. *(*KOLBE *appears at a table down stage, adding columns of numbers. He's in high spirits, although it's the end of the work day. He calls over his shoulder to an unseen assistant.)*

KOLBE   Soon! *(Back to work)* Times three, less the cost of newsprint, equals 16,670.

GAJOWNICZEK *(To* ZYMUNT*)*   We go on without you.

ALL *(*GAJOWNICZEK *to* ZYMUNT, ZYMUNT *to himself,* ANGELS *to* KOLBE.*)*
Go on.

KOLBE *(Adding another column)*   Plus seven plus eight. Times five, minus the ink. 16670. *(Pause)* That's peculiar. *(Another column)* Four into . . . plus two is 16670.
1-6-6-7-0.
1-6-6-7-0.
Why these numbers? Hairs on my head? Stumbles in a year? Varieties of laughter after a stumble?
1-6-6-7-0.
I live in Niepokalanow. I live in — the City of the Immaculate. I cannot suffer more than I suffer cheerfully at the hands of the Immaculate.

(GAJOWNICZEK *is not in pajamas — he's in prison clothes. He walks to* KOLBE *and addresses him.*)

GAJOWNICZEK   They've confiscated your city. It's your new address, brother. You live in Osweicim. You live in Auschwitz. (GAJOWNICZEK *rolls* KOLBE's *sleeve back. "16670" is printed across the priest's forearm.*) Maxmillian Mary Kolbe. Priest and publisher. How many letters in that name and title? 16670, I am sorry to say. (GAJOWNICZEK *kisses the priest on the forehead. He strips* KOLBE, *shaves his head, showers him, dresses him in a prisoner's uniform. Meanwhile.*)

FIRST ANGEL   And the wind falls off the night's high shelf when the massive dark makes a small move in its tight closet. The wind finds its way into every gaping. (MARY *with a cat's face and glasses enters and sits on* ZYMUNT's *chest.* MARY's *veil is seven-times pierced with a blue ribbon across the brow; the veil is braided behind her. The* SECOND ANGEL *holds* ZYMUNT's *head up. His eyes remain closed.*)

ZYMUNT   Myrrh?

SECOND ANGEL   Mary Mother of God, the cat-faced genius Notre Dame gargoyle, comes disguised as Zymunt's cat, Myrrh. She steals Zymunt's breath and makes it available to characters in the past. (MARY *puts her mouth over* ZYMUNT's, *takes breath, and breathes it back out over the scene. She steps back with the* ANGELS. ZYMUNT *wakes and looks at his clock;* KOLBE *looks at his forearm.*)

ZYMUNT *(To clock)*   Did you lick my eyelids?

KOLBE, ZYMUNT   The fire I am witnessing. The fire I am in. *(Blackout)*

Scene Two: Logs and Bodies

(ZYMUNT *is in the middle of the scene now, although he denies it. He's in a bathrobe, boxer shorts, and a sleeveless tee. He sits at what was* KOLBE's *table; the table is oriented differently now.* ZYMUNT *reads a newspaper and drinks coffee out of a very large cup. A barefoot* MARY, *still and ever cat-faced, rambles across the table top, occasionally looking down at what* ZYMUNT *is doing. Elsewhere,* KOLBE *and* GAJOWNICZEK *cross back and forth, loading invisible logs.)*

KOLBE   Is it summer solstice?

GAJOWNICZEK   No, you're dead by summer. You came in three days after Valentine's Day — you're gone by August. You're too strong now for this to be any later than spring.

KOLBE   I thought we were stacking logs for a solstice bonfire. *(ANGELS run in and lie down. They're the next logs lifted.)*

GAJOWNICZEK   These aren't logs. They're the bodies of the starved. We're on hard labor. We stack them. Children are kindling.

KOLBE   Why didn't I see this?

GAJOWNICZEK   The guards have just injected the phenol into your neck. These are visions you're having while dying. *(The hum of a bowed string. The humming continues through the blackout.)*

Scene Three: Two Crowns

(GAJOWNICZEK is off, and KOLBE is isolated. ZYMUNT is drinking coffee and reading, in the shadows; MARY *is with him.)*

KOLBE   At ten in Poland I see my father hung by the Russians. Rope is a string to play music on. Music's a math, a counting — but this sound is a counting to no quantity. The sounds are the components of words in a jumble, words that'll never be found. Warped the staff through which my mother flowed and her song bled away. Symbols lying in heaps in the margins. Traps for disease. This Boy — TB. Ground his sheets for newsprint.

GAJOWNICZEK *(Off)*   Max?

KOLBE   Ten years old I see my father hung, and when I go to sleep I have a dream.

GAJOWNICZEK   Max?

MARY   Sort it out, Zymunt. *(She crosses to* KOLBE, *and is in his dream. She produces a wreath of red flowers and a wreath of white.)* Which do you choose? The red or the white?

KOLBE   Both.

MARY   Both it is. *(She puts both wreaths on his head, playfully.)* I'm ten too. *(Suddenly serious)* But don't be fooled, Max.

KOLBE   By what?

MARY   By me. Because I've killed people. *(*KOLBE *takes* MARY*'s hand, and the couple turns upstage. They walk down a long road towards the blue-walled City of Mary.)*

Scene Four: City of Hope

*(*ZYMUNT *and his table are in a new position.* ZYMUNT *pours vodka into his coffee. His hand is bleeding.* GAJOWNICZEK *sits nearby, the alarm clock in his hands.)*

ZYMUNT

In the memoirs of the angel Freemason
It says that silence is a school
But that applies to a man, not a fool
A man's sense is in his mind, not his senses

When your cattle jump over your fences
Your milk and your meat jump too
Without what you were with, what are you?
You are passed as if there were a race on

On Chinese paper growing vines of black wisdom
    In the diary of a dead German poet
On cards in the wallets of heaven's few it says:
    If you cease to desire and be still
    The empire also will
But boy, you're divorced and you know it

(GAJOWNICZEK *bangs the clock down on the end of the table.* ZYMUNT *doesn't see him.*)

GAJOWNICZEK   There was no divorce. You never got married; that's not what you're getting at.

ZYMUNT *(Staring at the clock)*   Clock face is cat-mouthed gargoyle. Mouth of the clock where the whiskers meet in a whorl. *(*MARY *enters, crouches behind the clock, and draws breath.)*

GAJOWNICZEK   Sucked, sucked further, now through the face of the clock.

ZYMUNT   As if it weren't enough to wake up in the morning. *(He lurches forward; his head drains into the clock-face. Blackout.)*

Scene Five: 10 into 18

(GAJOWNICZEK *stands in a slow-moving line.* KOLBE *watches down-stage left.* ZYMUNT *crouches downstage right, shivering, reading his paper—a different paper now.)*

GAJOWNICZEK, ZYMUNT   10 into 18.

KOLBE   What?

GAJOWNICZEK   10 into 18.

KOLBE   Tell me your name. (GAJOWNICZEK *shows his number.)* Your name.

GAJOWNICZEK   Francis Gajowniczek.

ZYMUNT *(Reading from the paper, surprised to find this information there)*   When one prisoner tries to escape, ten are taken into Block 18, where they are starved and cremated.

KOLBE   Auschwitz.

ZYMUNT   That was a long time ago. The anvils go "r-r-ring" in my head and I was divorced a year ago. Let me think about divorce, man named Mary. Let me drink too much coffee, do the jumble, read the funnies. Let me hate the day in a swallow. Avoid my cat. Despise the world shown back from a black window at five A.M. The kitchen is purgatory because —

KOLBE   Math and music walk the same line. All math leads to heaven.

ZYMUNT   Because you are starving to death.

KOLBE   And from any column of numbers a number can be added or subtracted. You can take a letter from a row of letters and change a word. All words are letters waiting at different doors to death and heaven. You see my words, waiting so patiently? You cannot hear the doors open, but you know where they go.

ZYMUNT   You say:

KOLBE   I am a Catholic priest. I wish to die for that man. (Blackout)

Scene Six: The Escaped Man

(ZYMUNT's voice comes out of the darkness. Dawn is beginning to break.)

ZYMUNT   Set the alarm earlier to sleep less, see less, increase stupor, avoid falling through the "o" of o'clock. Slow time to where it has an atomic weight, super-heavy metal immobile on my plate. Head butting the iron-orange brow of the sun. Dawn. Word jumble. Paper stack at the stand diminishing. Caffeinosis. Liquor nesting in nerves and then fouling its nest. *(Lights up slowly. He's at the table; the table's in a new position.)* Jumble. *(*KOLBE *is discovered changing places with* GAJOWNICZEK. KOLBE *revolves into* GAJOWNICZEK's *place in line; they exchange letters of their names with every step. The exchange is simultaneous with* ZYMUNT's *lines.)* TISHUCAWS — Nine. HITAZU . . . THAUWI — AUCWI — AUSCHWI — *(*ZYMUNT *cuts himself off and crosses to a window.)* Thin old woman wakes across and down. The first horse-drawn milk truck to pass this way in fifty years rattles quarts of dawn-blood uphill at five. Thin woman in a cell down dying. AUKLAND.

KOLBE   Who escaped, Francis?

GAJOWNICZEK   I — I — I —

KOLBE   No, no — not —

GAJOWNICZEK   I have a family!

KOLBE   If none of us had ever been born, it would be so easy to change places.

GAJOWNICZEK   Don't change your mind. Take my place.

KOLBE   Keep this up, and they'll make it eleven. *(An* ANGEL *enters and hands* GAJOWNICZEK *his overcoat.* GAJOWNICZEK *separates himself, puts on the coat, and sticks a red poppy in his lapel.)*

GAJOWNICZEK *(Front)*   In 1975 I'm standing on a wooden platform in Krakow. We are remembering your name. One of my daughters, one of my many billion healthy daughters, is back from newspaper work in Mexico, and she wears two bone hands; they hang from her ears. I am meant to speak in commemoration, but I stop and hold the hands. *(*MARY *enters and stands facing* GAJOWNICZEK. *She wears bone-hand earrings.)*

KOLBE, ZYMUNT   Where is my suffering?

KOLBE   Who listens to my hands? Who accepts me into their prayers? *(Adding)* 1497777 plus equals. Ai. Numbers —

ZYMUNT   And the alphabet —

KOLBE   All a — jumble.

GAJOWNICZEK   I touch the bone hands hanging from my daughter's ears. *(He lifts MARY's earrings on his fingertips.)*

MARY   I listen.

ZYMUNT   But it's a ringing. *(A tense exhalation of air and KOLBE rolls against the wall; he scratches the numbers on his arm. ZYMUNT is isolated.)* Hid amongst the corpses for a night. Was so hungry they couldn't feel the motion of blood in my flesh as they carried me like wood. Rolled ghostly to the ditch. Crawled rain-snake to the fence. Smell-of-wire. Free in the woods. Epilepsy cold, covered in white sheet, snowfall. Now in Providence, Rhode Island, centuries later, out of sequence, I am jumbled back to the word: ESCAPEE. *(A ringing)* Got away and cannot live. Mary hide me. *(MARY spits.)*

FIRST ANGEL   Spat back through. *(The ringing is an alarm clock.)*

ZYMUNT   Mason angels invisible. They shined their seal, and now sneak behind the blinds. Work. *(ZYMUNT strips and takes a shower.)* Brain feels like it just ate rubber.

GAJOWNICZEK   Your hands are hanging Spanish from the ears of Gajowniczek's daughter. Anniversary. Your hands have gone through earth, come up bone, are ornament now. These are your phenol visions, Catholic. Be listened. You are being prayed.

ZYMUNT   Morning's suffering showering. Sense. Temperature and pattern of the water meeting the coffee-hot and pounding skin at zero.

KOLBE   One. One plus six plus six plus seven plus zero equals one.

ZYMUNT   Flesh is the zero envelope. The jumble hole. Is shape around the lack of — is shape against which sorrow showers. Holding nothing worth crying for. Mistakes at work. Mistakes with coffee, paper, shower, work. Newsprint on forearm.

GAJOWNICZEK   One.

KOLBE   10 into 18 equals one.

ZYMUNT *(Dries off, dresses. Shower sound gives way to bus commute, and typing.)*   Night into morning equals zero. In the holy city of Mary Militant — the town of Friars, Sodality of Mary — we typed against the fascists. Resisted once, and resisted twice, and were taken from Niepokalanow to Auschwitz in Osweicim. Escapee. For whom 18 was given as divisor to the 10. No. I am on a bus to lovely work. Cut and paste. On Tuesday with not a mark on my body. A young man. Morning breaking like starving in a sky canceled by the "x's" of the bridge's editing girders. Where will the meat of my sorrow be hung if I die when I die alone suicide when the hooks are hung with great canceled men? Room for my sorrow on the bare hooks of the abattoir bus.

ZYMUNT, GAJOWNICZEK, KOLBE   Concentration.

ZYMUNT *(Working the jumble)*   HOLOCAU — Mary, hide me. *(MARY draws her hand across ZYMUNT's forehead, mouth, throat, eyes, chest and stomach. He ages with each touch.)*

MARY   You're old. That's where you hide during the day.

GAJOWNICZEK   From a platform in Krakow in 1975 I see where they set the 10 of you in a room to starve. But the friars and refugees of Mary's city are used to penance and fasting. After two weeks, four are alive and you alone are conscious. You will not die, Kolbe. You set the dead in the earth like foundation logs. *(ZYMUNT arrives at work. On his desk, a computer made out of wood. The mouse is a literal mouse, in a small Hav-a-Hart trap.)*

ZYMUNT   Whoo, bad day.

GAJOWNICZEK   When you are thin enough, Mary plays the flute of you. *(The* ANGELS *enter and hold* KOLBE *up on their shoulders. He's stiff as a board; he faces up.* MARY *blows into his open mouth as if he were a flute, and flute music plays.)* The birds on the phone line in Krakow in 1975 are the same birds who stood on the barbed wire and watched. These birds are pouches of ash, and the cat won't molest them.

ANGELS
   The birds alighting as witnesses will never die
   Are nuns of the smoke
   The smoke from green wood
   The wives of the wire fly through smoke
   Light shabbat candles
   And return, alight

   They run smoke through their bodies
   They are palpitations of ash

   The witness birds will never die
   Are nuns of the smoke
   The smoke from green wood

SECOND ANGEL   Mary blows martyrdom through him, the air of all tenses.

GAJOWNICZEK   Because you would not die, they injected you with the chemical phenol. Needle pinching like a cat's tooth, cat breathing chemical into your neck. *(The* ANGELS *set* KOLBE *down. Mary produces a sword, and uses it to inject phenol into the priest's neck.)*

KOLBE   Pray that my love will be without limits.

ZYMUNT   Tag, shift, save, print. *(He presses the print button; he protects and feeds his mouse.)* Say cheese. *(Staring at the screen again)* Man in Rhode Island wakes to find his cat named Myrrh stealing his breath, cat licking Zymunt's lips, Myrrh the resin for anointing the dead, cat the creature that walks through tenses. Zymunt is carried with moonlight down the halls of heaven's secret society to Purgatory, where the cat is someone else, and where breath is played through the flute of a dead saint's body, the Kolbe flute. Wherever Zymunt steps, he falls through a jumble hole.

GAJOWNICZEK This is the land the sun mourns, this is the wake at which we watch under the light and reflected light. The moon's numbers are palimpsest but present in the daylight. Gajowniczek is passerby, with the passport of the cat.

MARY Mary Myrrh, cat and middle name, resembles conversation in a room where all are dying, where all good speech gathers to an act of lifting. Myrrh anoints your action, cat carries it back and forth through time, and Mary hides coins for you in words, because you will die last. She saves your labor. She prays for you to the Lord our God.

KOLBE Carry the one. Exposing the flesh. Carry the one. Up and over. Pour the lead. Am words, am plane, am in reverse, fevered, in love, hung from labor. X marks the spot, is the martyr meat-hook, is crosshairs indicating on Earth's head and fire my body through Satan's nickel-hot brain and explode into heaven. Pray that my love will be without limits. A cross I in my poverty borrow. Line, ribbon of heat, open ended sentence, sprung rhythm, pray that my love —

ANGELS
How do you handle it?
When are you over it?
You never wanted to travel this far

How do you answer it
Without an alphabet?
You never wanted to travel this far

UNA CARROÑA

(Rose of Lima)

Characters

Una Carroña was first performed at BACA in Brooklyn, as part of the series' premiere, March 1990, directed by Brian Mertes. Artistic director: Bonnie Metzger. Other series directors: Fritz Ertl, Thalia Field, Jennifer McDowall, Bonnie Metzger, and Randolyn Zinn. Cast: Minerva Scelva, Maria Porter, Adina Porter, Ileana Guilbert, Adriana Inchaustegui. Musician/Composer: Arturo Martinez. Vocalist: Klaudia Handszuh. Recitation: Silvia Nava. Production: Carise Skinner, David Burke, David Woolard, Michele Mayas, Barbara Chong, Jodi Feldman, Amanda Junquera, Kyle Chepulis, Stephen Kellam, Dawn Groenewegen.

(An empty dark room made out of wide wood planks. A knock on a door. 1, 2, 3, 4. 1, 2, 3, 4. A twelve-year-old girl slides into view backwards, sitting. She is in a cook's white clothes. There is a great red stain from her vagina. She drags herself to the upstage wall. She is dying quietly and alone in a ditch at night. Her eyes point in their final direction; see nothing; reflect death.)

GIRL   Holy Saint Rose, oh Rose, sing for us. A sad song of mourning, a march for the just. In the dust, in the heat, tell the tale by the well. Like a thief in the night, drag their souls down to hell. *(A woman is revealed; she is under interrogation. She has a shirt on but no skirt. She feels humiliation, sitting in her underwear before an unseen audience of men.)*

WOMAN   I deny my earlier statement and damn my soul to hell in the presence of Rose of Lima. Rose of Lima. *(1, 2, 3, 4. ROSE enters and kneels, elsewhere.)*

ROSE   Cannot be alone enough. So many dying alone. Cannot repent enough. So much flesh for the devil to set his purchase in. *(Rose's MOTHER enters and knocks, with a different sound.)*

MOTHER   Rose?

WOMAN   The night of November 16.

GIRL   Rose?

WOMAN   I did *not* see the men cross through the priests' gate before the Oscar Romero residence at the UCA. I do not name the residence pointedly, that is the name by which I know it.

ROSE *(Praying)*   I will please them. I will please them. Only let me suffer effectively. *(MOTHER exits.)*

WOMAN   I know who you are. I know this man is a colonel from my own country. I have never been out of El Salvador in my life. I do not like this city. Yes, back to undo my story. *(MOTHER enters with a dress over one arm. Knocks.)*

MOTHER   Rose?

ROSE   Mother, I am praying.

GIRL   Rose?

WOMAN   The men I did not see in combat fatigues had not come by this campus earlier to ransack the files of the priests. Has my family eaten? Are they still in the hall?

MOTHER   I have a pretty dress.

WOMAN   They found enough to kill them for. I'm sorry. They found enough to prosecute them for. But they did not prosecute. I am saying that of course they would have been justified in killing them. Because they called for land reform and food. Which is to say they quoted the gospel from the pulpit. Surely unnatural and incendiary. The six of them. The six Jesuits. I am damning my soul to hell with these words. Look at me when I'm lying to you.

ROSE   Surely there is something I own already, far more beautiful than any dress. (MOTHER *exits. 1, 2, 3, 4 knocks on the door, as she crosses.*)

WOMAN   I remember more clearly the incidents from farther back. The incidents that *other* people have sworn never happened. Those I am allowed to know. The four church women at the roadblock. Something comical about religious women, women in a group. Something goofy. (*Four nuns enter. They each lift one foot off the ground as if they are about to fly, and then they drop.*) Goofy like felled birds. How stupid these women were — to stand, or to run. To be here. And surely Romero who never stood at the altar never fell forward into his leaping blood. If he had, it would have been because he was instructing peasants how to make weapons out of the corn cobs they steal from the pig troughs out behind the army barracks. Nothing happens. No one falls. And no saints in heaven can suffer enough to absolve the sin of my recantation. I hate this city. Saint Rose! (MOTHER *enters, knocks. A boy, just a boy, in a suit, is in tow.*)

MOTHER   Rose?

GIRL   Rose?

ROSE   I am nearly the Rose of Lima now, mother.

MOTHER   I have a groom, Rose. A boy to marry.

ROSE   Mother, I am praying.

WOMAN   This is the last little bit of what I did not see that night.

MOTHER   This is the third time you have refused me. *(She exits with the groom. 1, 2, 3, 4 as they go.* ROSE *lets her dress off her shoulders; she is wearing a corset of thorns. She tightens the corset. 1, 2, 3, 4)*

ROSE   Not come in. Not anything. Cannot be simple enough. *(1, 2, 3, 4)*

WOMAN   They knocked. And one of the priests opened the door. I live in El Salvador. One of the priests opened the door. I did not see these things. Priests came quietly, assuming it was more questioning. 70,000 dead in El Salvador in ten years. *Ten.* Rose. *(*MOTHER *enters.)*

MOTHER   Rose.

GIRL   Rose? I won't ask again.

MOTHER   Rose. We have lost all our money. Your father's mines have failed. Will you help us?

ROSE *(Cutting crosses into her upper arms with a knife)*   Of course, mother. It is in me to do that. I will take in sewing.

WOMAN   70,000. And the priests out there. The moist night flat. Lined up on a road of chipped stone.

ROSE   Everyone needs new clothes. I will not take new clothes. But I

will make them. Dresses for girls. Special occasions. Funerals. First funerals. So many die thin. Narrow dresses. Narrow shroud. So much
agony. Go away. *(MOTHER exits. 1, 2, 3, 4)*

WOMAN   They knocked.

ROSE   There was an answer.

WOMAN   The priest came to the door.

ROSE   And went back to get the others.

WOMAN   They gathered.

ROSE   Stood ready to discourse, to answer all questions in the high
quick desperate voices the army likes. Each one was shot in the head.

WOMAN   What is the death of priests and nuns when so many die? Ex-
cept that priests and nuns are dressed in our flag, in the people's flag. The
black flag of anarchy. Love and conscience being above the laws. The terrible, brutal, mortally threatening anarchy of love. The poison, the pirate
black love.

ROSE   They were dragging the bodies to the ditches when they heard
the cook and her daughter evading moonlight inside. The soldiers caught
them both, and shot them between the legs. They bled to death slowly;
crawled to each other and spooned.

WOMAN   The men combed the area for other witnesses, but found
none. They assumed that the camouflage fatigues they wore made them
as invisible as gods, when they so plainly made them the visible arm of the
mystical body of the devil. I was yards away. I was praying to St. Rose. I
saw none of this. I saw no one die. I did not cross the street after the soldiers left to enter and close the eyes of the cook's daughter. *(1, 2, 3, 4)*

ROSE   Paul, come in, but don't let mama in. *(1, 2, 3, 4)* Paul, come in. I
have set up the room for a game. *(1, 2, 3, 4)* Paul, come in. We can play

hermit. I am praying to Catherine of Siena. *(1, 2, 3, 4)* Paul, come in. I am ten years old again. I am alive. I did not die at thirty-one, killed by strict penance, killed trying to mortify my flesh past the reach of the devil. You are seven. you are my brother. *(1, 2, 3, 4)* Paul, come in. We will play hermit in the roses. We will make a perfect world. Paul, come in! *(A* SOLDIER *bursts in. Surprised and confused)*

SOLDIER *(To* ROSE*)*   Who are you?

WOMAN   I saw nothing. And even so, I saw this, this happened.

WOMAN and ROSE
     The scene is a road in a jungle at night
     As wild as a young lover's heart
     Drizzle and music and laughter, then fright
     As the bushes by the roadblock part

     Four girls in a jeep step quick to the ground
     Their old weathered hands in the air
     They stare like cougars and the M-16s pound
     The power of death through their hair

     A man in his prime is folding, unfolding
     His hands and his love for us all
     As he offers his guests the bread he is holding
     The assassin walks down the hall

     Six in a building named for this man
     Are summoned by a drumming so bold
     Four nuns, an archbishop, six priests, many thousands
     How many can the ditches of El Salvador hold?

     Una carroña
     It's once over lightly
     The moon shining brightly
     On the nightly quota

     Una carroña
     Another dead Jesuit

I like the sound of it
On the Voice of America

Una carroña
The rot and stagnation
The beer and malaria
The abomination

Una carroña
Another dead nun
The work's never done
When you join the militia

Holy Saint Rose, oh Rose, sing for us
A sad song of mourning, a march for the just
In the dust, in the heat, tell the tale by the well
Then like a thief in the night drag their souls down to hell

Una carroña
It's once over lightly
The moon shining brightly
On the nightly quota

Una carroña
Stack them up at the wall
Cut their tendons, make them crawl
Across the arena

Una carroña
Slaughter the mother
Then run down the daughter
Shoot her in the vagina

Una carroña
Hide your badges, hide your badges
Cover fire flashes
Stars and bars in aurora

Una carroña
The lightning of Zion
In the eyes of the icon
Of Saint Rose of Lima

WOMAN   And the final words of the priest were:

ROSE *(Rising. Directly to the soldier)*   Esta es una injusticia. Es una carroña!

THISTLE

(Rose of Lima)

Characters

Thistle premiered at the House of Charity in Spokane, Washington, October 23, 1998, presented by St. Michael's Institute, under the auspices of the Loyola Project. Directed by the playwright and Jack Bentz, S.J. Loyola Project director: Jack Bentz. Cast: Ryan Booth, S.J., Ann Gillum, Lorenzo Herman, Linsey Morse, James Nolte, S.J., Jesus Palomino, S.J., Chris Palmer, Bryan Pham, S.J., Liezl Rebugio, Tami Rotchford. Musicians: Ann Gillum, Bob Beaumier, Jack Bentz. Production: Eileen Anderson, Dale Blick, Pedro Bautista, Sam Calderon, Rick Conboy, S.J., Joe Conwell, S.J., John Enslin, S.J., Cliff Erdman, Mike Farrell, Dan Greer, S.J., Jerry Hayes, S.J., Ryan Hendricks, Craig Hightower, S.J., Bill James, Mike Johnson, Joe Lingan, S.J., Diana Martinez, Raul Matamoros, S.J., Sean McCann, S.J., Tom Mulligan, Chu Ngo, S.J., Don Ojala, Jason S. Pankow, Tan Pham, S.J., Cec Sheoships, Vincent P. Scott, S.J., Duane Sessions, Don Simmonsen, Oliver Summers, Jeff Wilson, Eric Zuckerman, S.J., and the patrons of the House of Charity. A Dance Version of the play was developed with Carolyn Silberman (Department of Dance) and students at Santa Clara University. Juan Carlos Mendizabal composed the electronic score. Ms. Silberman choreographed. Presented in connection with Santa Clara's Institute on Justice in the Arts, March 1996.

Massacre in El Mozote
Jurisdiction of Meanguera, Morazán
El Salvador

IX Anniversary: December 11, 12 and 13, 1990
Testimony: Sister Rufina Amaya Marquez, forty-nine years old

Testimony

"Everything began when Mr. Marcos Diaz, who had the biggest shop in El Mozote, was told in Gotera (the capital of the department of Morazán) when he was on his way to buy some goods, that he should buy two truckloads of food instead of one, because the Army was not going to allow any more food into the town as they were planning a military operation there in the North of Morazán. The Army told him that he should gather all the townspeople together in the municipal center of the town.

"I was in Isidra Claros' house on the 10th of December when the Army arrived in the afternoon and forced us out of the houses and ordered us to lay face down on the ground in front of Mr. Marco Diaz's house. They made us get up about seven o'clock at night and took all of the money we had on us as well as all our jewelry, and they sent us back inside the houses. They told us not even to stick our noses out because if we did, they would shoot us. No one went out, not even to take care of our physical necessities.

"We awakened in the houses on the 11th. At five in the morning they took us out of our homes and made us line up in the plaza, one line of men, one of women and one of children. At seven in the morning a helicopter arrived and so they made us all go back inside the house of Alfredo Marquez, but the men they separated from us and put them inside the church. After this, the soldiers came in and began threatening us with their knives and rifles, telling us that they were going to let the men go, but that we had to tell them where we kept the arms first. We told them that we were unarmed. They then went to where the men were being held, tied them up, blindfolded them, and stood on top of them beating them. After this, they took them out in pairs and killed them.

"All of this I saw through a little hole in the window of the house where we women were being held. Some of the men were taken first to their homes and were ordered to turn over all the money they had, but they too were brought back and killed and their bodies thrown in the convent of the church.

"After this the soldiers arrived where we women were and they took out all the young girls that were there; their mothers were held back, crying and screaming for them to leave the girls alone. But the soldiers just kicked them and punched them with their rifles, and the poor ladies just stayed there crying for their daughters. Some women, elderly and blind, were crying and screaming to be set free; the soldiers didn't want to deal with them and so they took them out and they never returned.

"Later they continued taking people out in groups, and evidently were killing them because we could hear the shots. At five in the afternoon of this day the 11th, they took out a group of twenty-two women where I was being held, and brought them out in front of the house of Israel Marquez. As we arrived at the *pila* and the front door of the house, you could see how the blood was running. I felt very anxious, because I knew that they were going to kill me and I had four children that I had to leave behind when they divided us into groups of women, children and men. Well, upon seeing this river of blood, the women began to cry and scream.

"I, as I remembered my children — Christino Amaya Claros of nine years, Maria Dolores Amaya Claros of five years, Martha Liliam Amaya Claros of three years and Maria Isabel Amaya Claros of eight months — I fell to my knees and prayed and begged God to save me from death or to pardon the sins that I had committed. At that moment I crawled to a nearby apple tree and pulled down one of the branches in order to hide myself, but the soldiers were still there in front and on all sides of the house. From there I could see when they rounded up all the women again and put them into the house, one of them carrying a small child in her arms. They brought them into the house and killed them. They continued killing them in this way, group by group. When they were bringing forward the group of women that I had been in, I felt the desire to give myself up and let them kill me. But at the same time I remembered that God had already saved me because they hadn't seen me.

"The soldiers then commented, 'OK, we've finished with the old women and men, now only the children are left.'

"At about seven o'clock at night a soldier arrived to tell them to set the house on fire, and so they did. You could then hear that there was a child crying out from the flames as the house was burning. One soldier told the other to shoot the child so that it would stop crying. A group of soldiers then sat down in front of where I was hiding and were saying: 'Now only the children are left, I don't know what we should do with them.' Another said to him, 'Yeah, but the colonel said that we weren't to leave anyone alive, and we are fulfilling an order because this is a scorched earth operation.'

"After this a few of the soldiers retreated, but several groups of them stayed and there were others in all of the dead end streets. You could hear some of the children screaming and crying, but you couldn't hear any shots because they were killing them with knives. The soldiers that stayed were commenting that they were already killing the children with knives and strangling them.

"I thought about leaving but I was afraid they might see me. Then, the light from the burning house was attracting some animals, dogs and calves, and sparks were falling on me because the house almost completely burned down. Around twelve at night I took advantage of the fact that these animals had arrived to play in the light of the fire, and so I sneaked out, crawling on my hands and knees between the legs of the calves, grabbing my dress and my hair so that they wouldn't notice that I was a person. I finally arrived at a fence and went through, and at this point they couldn't see me, and I fell on my knees crying and praying, I felt so bewildered and confused. I then continued crawling through the bushes so that they wouldn't see me, and I arrived at a small clearing with houses called La Chumpa. As I went crawling through some cactus plants, some soldiers saw me and started shooting at me like crazy. But they didn't get me, and I could hear them saying, 'Look there's a woman over there' . . . 'No, there's nothing there' . . . 'Yeah, there is, there she goes' . . . 'No way, the dead are scaring you, there's nothing over there.'

"And so they got scared and went running. I had stayed down with my face against the ground covering myself with some cactus plants, and I didn't walk around much because I was afraid to go any further down the hill. I woke up on the 12th. On this day I could hear the screams of the little girls on the hills who were saying, 'Don't kill me, ay, don't kill me.' They were raping and killing them.

"Among these cactus plants I stayed the whole day. At about six in the evening I went crawling face down in the cactus plants because if I stood up they would see me. When I arrived down the hill in a small village called El Jocote, I didn't even have my dress on anymore, it got completely ripped off while I was crawling in the bush, my arms and my stomach were all bloody from so much crawling. I arrived at the house where my father lived but there was no one there because they had fled. I looked for some clothes and found some of my father's pants and a sweater and put them on.

"During the day I stayed in the bush and at night I slept in the little house owned by Andres Chicas. After eight days of this, on the 17th, the wife of Andres arrived while I was there. She was with some girls and they were bringing corn. They found me there and told me that we should go to some caves where they were hiding and so I went off with them. We were fleeing together for quite some time, until the time when I went to the Colomoncagua refugee camp in Honduras. Today I live in Segundo Montes City."

A: Open

(A girl, a red brick, a radio. The radio's a portable, it sits on the brick; the GIRL *is a Santa Clara student. She has trouble getting a station — she fiddles with the dial, then the antenna; she finally changes the relationship of her body to the box. She moves closer, then further away, her arms out, then by her side. Her movements become a dance. Sounds drift. Taped sound falls to a live, stylized song that represents the crosscurrents of signals.)*

RADIO
    A kind of place that —
    Ago —
    Early morning —
    My baby —
    For the rest —
    My love —
    Treating me like —
    My heart —

(A woman in the clothes of a Salvadoran agricultural worker appears behind a desk. She wears headphones and speaks into a mic; she is broadcasting. The GIRL *doesn't see the woman yet — only hears her.)*

BROADCASTER   You found me.

GIRL   Says who?

BROADCASTER   Radio Venceremos out of Morazán in El Salvador,
1982

GIRL   Now isn't then.

BROADCASTER   It's through you.

GIRL   You're too far away.

BROADCASTER
Your heart's a crystal
Through which ghost radio focuses
Stay still
We will come through you
Stay still until we tune
Then move again
Move

(The signal is clear. The GIRL *turns and sees the* BROADCASTER.*)*

GIRL   You come from —

BROADCASTER   Radio signal never goes. The guerrillas in El Salvador
ran a mobile radio station out of caves and tunnels years ago. The signals
drift and bounce forever between the stars.

GIRL   Why 1982?

BROADCASTER   A record is skipping. It's stuck there. *(A recording)*

RUFINA'S VOICE   Everything began when Mr. Marcos Diaz, who had
the biggest shop in El Mozote — *(A skip and this repeats several times.)*

GIRL   What begins?

BROADCASTER   This is the sworn testimony of Sister Rufina Amaya Marquez regarding the massacre of 1,100 men women and children in the Thistle, Morazán Province, El Salvador; the killing takes place over three days: December 11, 12 and 13, 1981. This is testimony, child.

GIRL   How did you find me in Santa Clara?

BROADCASTER   You found *me*. The way you moved, you moved right to me.

> Your heart is a crystal
> Lanced by our signal
> Neither of us has a choice in this

GIRL *(Speaking)*   Get the record to stop skipping.

BROADCASTER   Then you will hear her whole story.

GIRL   How do we keep it from skipping?

BROADCASTER   You're listening. Your attention is the bump that un-sticks it.

> El Mozote, the Thistle, is a town in Morazán
> Where a thousand people were slain
> A woman, Rufina, testifies, solo
> None of the others remain
>
> Radio lances your heart
> We start
> Radio lances your heart
> We start

B: Fourteen Stations

1. EVERYTHING BEGINS

(Scene title projected and announced. Diaz walks down a road, no sound but a wooden clapping; Diaz is stopped by a man who holds him by the shoulders and whispers into his ear. Silence and a freeze at the gesture of the whisper.)

BROADCASTER   Two sentences:
(The BROADCASTER *reaches out to start a record.* RUFINA *comes up behind her, puts her hand over the* BROADCASTER*'s, and co-narrates. The* BROADCASTER *trails off. Music begins with the speech; Diaz and the Official move. Townspeople set out chairs.)*

BROADCASTER, RUFINA   Everything began when Mr. Marcos Diaz, who had the biggest shop in El Mozote, was told in Gotera when he was on his way to buy some goods, that he should buy two truckloads of food instead of one, because the army was not going to allow any more food in the town as they were planning a military operation there in the north of Morazán. The army told him that he should gather all the townspeople together in the center of El Mozote.
(Music and speech stop together. Everyone sits as in a game of musical chairs. No chair for the GIRL.*)*

GIRL *(Recognizing the woman with the* BROADCASTER*)*   That woman is Rufina Amaya. Where will she sit? I'll get her a chair. *(She slowly turns away and is fixed in a gesture of reaching. Blackout)*

2. I WAS

(Scene title projected in the dark.)

BROADCASTER   Radio Venceremos. "I was."
(Lights up. RUFINA *alone in a chair. She joins in on the underlined phrases.)*
I was in Isidra Claros' house on the 10th of December when the Army

arrived in the <u>afternoon</u> and forced us out of the house and ordered us to <u>lie face down on the ground</u> in front of <u>Mr. Diaz's</u> house.

(RUFINA stands; her chair is handed away by an Army Officer. RUFINA is joined by three Townspeople. They lie down three times in three different ways. One: RUFINA speaks and they go to the ground.)

RUFINA   I was, then lay face down.
(They stand back up.)
I was in —
(Two: they drop as if thrown down; they stand back up.)
I was —
(Three: they lie down slowly, as if shot through the back and falling through water.)

BROADCASTER   They made us get up about seven o'clock at night and took all of our money, jewelry, sent us back inside the houses. Not to come out or they would shoot us. No one did, not even to take care of physical necessities. *(They each in turn get up and leave, separately, some stiff-jointed, unsure whether they should go or stay. The GIRL comes forward and takes a handful of dirt.)*

GIRL
    I will keep a handful of dirt
    From before anything happens here
    My heart is radio crystal
    In my heart is the thistle
    In my pocket a fist of dirt
    From before anything happens

3. WE AWAKENED

(Title projected and announced. Then, still in the dark.)

BROADCASTER   We awakened, those of us who could sleep at all, we awakened early. The cows and goats unmilked too long. They complained as long as they could then stood low-headed, mask-faced, watching. *(Lights up and the GIRL has a cow mask on. The BROADCASTER comes out from behind the table, and joins the Townspeople.)*

GIRL   They woke up in the houses on the 11th. At five they took them out and lined them up, separate lines for the men, the women, and the children. *(The Townspeople dance, breaking off and recombining: six breaks to four and two, five and one, six individuals, three and three, and finally three pairs of two . . . One pair stands as men, with hands bound behind their backs, one pair stands as women, with hands bound in front, and one pair stands as children — hands empty and heads down.)* Women and children then crowded together into the one house, men to the church. *(The women and children gather in a tight cluster, and the men move downstage. The GIRL, in her mask, listens closely to the group of women and children, as if through a wall.)* The soldiers say: "We will let the men go, but you have to tell us where you keep the arms."

WOMEN and CHILDREN   We-are-un-armed. *(The men are blindfolded. Fingers drawn across one man's throat.)*

GIRL   The tendons in their necks part with the sound of sawed guitar strings. The awful chord is gorgeous, played in a martyr's key. *(She takes off her mask.)* For thinking so prettily, I will pay. *(Blackout)*

4. ALL OF THIS I SAW

(Title projected but not announced. Lights up to discover the BROADCASTER behind her table, reading from a document.)

BROADCASTER   All of this I saw through a little hole in the window of the house where the women were being held. *(RUFINA stands apart from a bound Man. The Man tries to turn his face to hers, can't. Tries to free his arms, can't. Tries to cry out, can't.)*

RUFINA   All of this I saw —

GIRL   All of this I heard through ghost radio Venceremos pirating the Santa Clara band. *(RUFINA and the Man dance. The Man takes a weaker part; RUFINA saves him from the floor.)*

GIRL and BROADCASTER
All of this I saw
Animals unmilked and starving
Dancing in the famine moon
Lovers and brothers cut down too soon
All of this I saw through a hole

All of this I saw
I saw more when the
Sun rose, as it will (as it will)
This is happening still
I saw, I saw through a hole

(The GIRL is forced to wear the coat of a soldier; she is handed a bayonet. She is pushed into the narrative against her will. She moves towards the Man as he dances with RUFINA.)

BROADCASTER   All of this. Some of the men were taken first to their houses and —

GIRL   No. No.

BROADCASTER   Were ordered to turn over all the money they had, but they too were brought back and —

GIRL   No.

BROADCASTER   And killed, their bodies thrown into the convent of the church.

GIRL *(Her bayonet at the Man's throat)*   No.

RUFINA   This happens. This is the sound. *(The GIRL cuts the throat in silence; the Man's exhalation is the only sound. The GIRL reels away and stares at what she has done.)*

RUFINA, GIRL   A hole. *(Blackout)*

5. AFTER THIS

(In a twilight, the GIRL *— dressed as herself again — tunes the radio with her body. Lights fade back to black and the title appears. A breath. The sense of a new section beginning. Light. The* BROADCASTER *reads at her table, and the* GIRL *reads over her shoulder.)*

BROADCASTER   "After This." After this the soldiers came to where we women were.

GIRL   The young women. The old women.

BROADCASTER   The young women, exact in their fright; the old women superb at keening.

GIRL   Removed. *(*RUFINA *is discovered standing on a chair. She releases an imaginary object from her right hand — the girls; her left hand tightens to a clutch around nothing — the old women.)*

BROADCASTER   The women between youth and age, between sitting and standing, between life and death, remained.

RUFINA   Those taken, never returned. *(Blackout)*

6. LATER THEY CONTINUED

(Title projected and announced. RUFINA, *the* GIRL *and the* BROADCASTER *dance together; gracefully pass a length of red ribbon between them.)*

RUFINA'S VOICE *(On tape)*   At five in the afternoon on this day, the 11th, they took a group of twenty-two of us women. *(A burst of static. the dancers fall out of sync. They adjust their postures to receive signal; static subsides; they continue. A rat enters and takes one end of the ribbon in its mouth; he pulls it away, slowly.)* Outside you could see how the blood was running. *(The women hide their hands in each others' bodies. Their mouths by each others' ears, they whisper, audibly.)*

RUFINA, GIRL, BROADCASTER   Upon seeing this river of blood, the women began to cry and scream. *(This sentence is repeated, volume increasing to no more than a conversational level, as the lights fade.)*

7. I AS I REMEMBERED

(Title projected but not announced. In the dark, the sounds of a children's game. The BROADCASTER has her hand over the mic. RUFINA walks a few steps, stops to look back, drops to her knees to pray, and then covers herself, hiding on the ground. The GIRL tries to hide with her — tries to offer comfort. RUFINA pushes her away, gently, authoritatively. Three children sit stage left, cross-legged. They start to play an elaborate concentration game, involving claps and snaps. RUFINA rises and repeats her cycle of motions — walking, praying, hiding. The GIRL tries to enter the circle of children, but can't. She sits in a chair, apart. Music.)

RUFINA   I as I remembered my children

CHILDREN
    Christino Amaya Claros, nine
    Maria Dolores Amaya Claros, five
    Martha Liliam Amaya Claros, three
    Maria Isabel Amaya Claros, eight months

RUFINA
    I fell to my knees and prayed
    Forgiveness for the sins I've made
    I pulled down the branch of an apple tree
    And begged my lord to save me

(Clapping stops abruptly with the last line of the lyric.)

GIRL   The soldiers were. I was. The soldiers were on all sides. They killed the women in groups. *(A smiling MOTHER appears stage right. She encourages RUFINA as if she were a baby.)*

MOTHER   Come here. Come here, baby. Don't hold on — you can walk. *(RUFINA starts to crawl towards her.)*

RUFINA   When they were bringing forward the group of women I had
been in, I felt the desire to give myself up and let them kill me.

MOTHER   Come on. *(The Children in the circle begin to crawl too.)*

RUFINA   But at the same time I remembered that God had already
saved me because they hadn't seen me. *(All crawl now as if they are
grown women in distress. The three stage left collapse;* RUFINA *remains
up, one hand extended to the* MOTHER. *The* MOTHER *leaves, imperson-
ally.* RUFINA *quickly hides herself. Blackout)*

8. THE SOLDIERS THEN COMMENTED

*(Title projected, not announced. Lights up. Four Soldiers, facing for-
ward, a staggered line. They dance in a round. One initiates a sequence
of moves which suggests heavy manual labor — the lifting up and laying
down of burdens. The* GIRL *is one of the Soldiers; she can't complete all
the repetitions. She falls, exhausted. When the round is finished, the*
BROADCASTER *reads.)*

BROADCASTER   The soldiers then commented: "OK, we've finished
with the old women and men, now only the children are left." *(Blackout)*

9. AT ABOUT SEVEN O'CLOCK AT NIGHT

(Title projected and read. In the dark.)

TWO SOLDIERS   Set that house on fire.

RUFINA   Thin green sap expands at the rate of kerosene. *(*RUFINA, *hiding on the floor center stage, is gradually revealed by the red light of a rising fire. All around her, soldiers stand immobile. Stage left, the*
BROADCASTER *holds her hand over the* GIRL's *mouth; the* GIRL
whimpers like expanding sap.) No. The voice of one of the children. I
don't know this child.

RUFINA and BROADCASTER   Please.

BROADCASTER   Please: don't make Rufina move. *(The* GIRL *bites the* BROADCASTER'*s hand; the* BROADCASTER *sucks the wound.)*

GIRL *(Whispering audibly)*   Rufina.

RUFINA   Do I know this child?

SOLDIERS and GIRL *(Whispering)*   Mama.

RUFINA   I don't know —

GIRL   She knows. *(The* GIRL *approaches* RUFINA, *slowly.)*

BROADCASTER   She can't move.

RUFINA   Voice walking towards me with the solidity of a horse. Roan. Coat of fire. A saint, all bone, insane on Voice's back, armed, prepared to identify — me. Globe-eyed horse — foam lunged, from fire, sniffs the ground. Twenty five percent of Apocalypse walks up on me from the left saying "mama."

GIRL   Rufina. Rufina. *(She's almost there. The* SOLDIERS *sit in a circle around* RUFINA, *facing out. The* GIRL *crouches in shadow, reaching out.)*

SOLDIER ONE   Only children left —

SOLDIER TWO   In the last house.

SOLDIER THREE   What should we do?

SOLDIER TWO   Some of them are really cute. *(Each produces a small toy — an orange, plastic horse. They set the horses down.)*

SOLDIER THREE   It would be a shame to kill them. *(Slow, highly controlled tumbles around the toys, weight on hands. They are contemplating.* RUFINA *repeats, rapidly and without voice: "My children! My children!" We hear the click of her tongue.)*

BROADCASTER *(Into mic)*   Rufina in the fire's light, buried in cold worm soil, spoke with breath contracted. My children! Words shrinking to ice.

SOLDIER ONE   Yeah, but the Colonel said we weren't to leave —

SOLDIER TWO   Anyone alive.

SOLDIER THREE   Operativo tierra arrasada.

GIRL   Scorched Earth Operation.

BROADCASTER   The apple tree did not catch fire because Rufina was in a world of ice.

RUFINA   It took two men to pull the baby from me.

BROADCASTER   One corpse found with a plastic horse strangely perfect in the pocket of the degrading pants.

GIRL   She scooped a hole — in which — to catch — her sobbing. *(Blackout)*

10. AFTER THIS THE SOLDIERS

(Title projected, not read. The BROADCASTER *and the* GIRL *are seen holding out a three-by-nine-foot length of red silk; they hold the length between them.* RUFINA *cuts the cloth into three equal pieces, slowly, slowly.)*

RUFINA   After this some soldiers retreated, but the elite continued working in the dark. Because I was so near, and so still, I could hear their moves through the roots of the tree. My hands were over my ears to shut out the screams, the roots became my fingers and I heard anyway. No shots. They were killing them with knives. We will dress ourselves in silence for a new ceremony. We will clothe ourselves with silence for a marriage to this place. *(The women move with the cut silk. Blackout)*

(Title projected and announced. RUFINA, *so tired, lies alone center stage, the red silk gathered around her as a blanket.)*

RUFINA . . . But I was afraid they might see me. Sparks flew down on me from the last house burning. *(The* GIRL *appears on a ladder. She sprinkles red sparks over* RUFINA. *A dog, a cow and a goat appear, singing. They dance.)*

ANIMALS
  Fascinated by the light
  The animals come to play
  Dogs and cows and goats
  Fascinated by the light

  Who suckles the udders to relieve them?
  The animals nurse each other
  They are drunk on strange milk
  The animals suckle each other
  Fascinated by the light

  The killing is nearly over
  The light is fascinating
  Skeletal pup and calf and kid
  The refugee escapes
  In their play

(The ANIMALS *begin to move in concert. They head off, stage left.* RUFINA *begins to mirror their actions. The* GIRL *comes down from the ladder and tries to mirror as well, but* RUFINA *pushes her back.)*

RUFINA Stay. *(The* GIRL *sits stage right and watches. The* ANIMALS *leave.* RUFINA *prays.)*

BROADCASTER The animals, delirious with hunger and lightheaded in the glow and myrrh of the crematory, gave me cover. I pretended I was a dog, and moved by their flanks. Through the fence of midnight and onto the side of the next day, eternal. I prayed and prayed. *(A* SOLDIER *enters and lies between* RUFINA *and the* GIRL. *He levels a rifle at* RUFINA. *The* GIRL *starts to rise.)*

RUFINA and BROADCASTER   Stay. *(The* GIRL *stays.)*

SOLDIER   I see something over there. Nothing? Yes, there she is. *(A drum indicates gunshots.)*

GIRL and BROADCASTER   She is the Witch of El Mozote, la llarona! The bullets turn to water. *(Blackout)*

12. AND SO THEY GOT SCARED

(Projected and announced. In the dark.)

BROADCASTER   And so they got scared and went running. I ran the other way. I awoke the next day, on the 12th of December, and ran again. *(Sun. A beautiful, clear day.* RUFINA *and the* GIRL *run together in a circuit around the stage.)*

RUFINA   Birdsong. *(And this is heard. A Bird appears on a high branch.* RUFINA *and the* GIRL *stop abruptly, to listen.)*

BIRD
    Running by a hill called La Cruz
    Rufina heard the girls
    It had taken this many days
    For the soldiers to finish

    "Ay, don't kill me, don't kill me, ay ay"
    They resisted like birds in their hands
    As birds they were murdered
    As girls, raped
    The song stayed high in the trees *(Speaking)*

One girl sang through the ordeal, a simple song, a song of her town. A song they couldn't take from her. They shot her in the chest and the song still came. They had to put the metal of a knife's blade between her heart and mouth.

RUFINA, GIRL, BIRD
  The stars are invisible
  In all this sunlight
  But I know they are there
  They are nails

  Invisible nails
  Hammering finity
  My carpenter builds a day
  They are nails

  A structure of innocence
  Thorned to the sky
  Boards joined at the pain
  He and I
  La Cruz in the sky
  He and I *(Blackout)*

13. AMONG THESE CACTUS PLANTS

(Title projected, not announced. A breath; the sense of a new section. The GIRL *draws water from a well.* RUFINA *pulls herself slowly across the stage.)*

BROADCASTER   Among these cactus plants I stayed the whole day. Went crawling. *(A discovery)* My dress is ripped!

CHORUS
  Among these cactus plants, during the day
  What happened here? What happened here?
  The thorn and the thistle along the way
  What happened here? What happened here?
  The events are gone, the witness lives on
  The roses know all that there is to say

(The GIRL *catches up with* RUFINA *and washes her feet, gets her dressed.)*

BROADCASTER   I arrived at the house where my father lived but there was no one there because they had fled. I looked for some clothes and found some of my father's pants and a sweater and put them on. *(Blackout)*

14. DURING THE DAY

BROADCASTER *(Announcing)*   Last one: "During the Day."
(The GIRL *and one or two others are making low altars out of bricks and plates. The only light on stage comes from candles at the shrines. Candles appear from elsewhere in a dark, danced procession.)*

CHORUS
    Among these cactus plants, during the day
    Filled with bones, filled with bones
    I walk among them in every direction
    How dry they are, how dry they are
    My words make skin, put spirit in
    Over the desert, the breath of resurrection

    We live again
    Bones and skin
    Spirit kisses
    Resurrection in

    We live again
    We live again
    The land is ours
    Oh my people

RUFINA *(Speaking)*
    During the day
    I stayed in the bush
    At night I slept

In the house of Andres Chicas
Girls brought corn
We lived in caves.
We fled together.
Today I live in Segundo Montes City.

C: Close

(The sounds of a helicopter)

GIRL   Where did she go?

BROADCASTER   Where she lives.

GIRL   Your signal is weak.

BROADCASTER   We're done.

GIRL   What else?

BROADCASTER   The bullet casings were all stamped "U.S. Army." You could hold them in your hand. The Atlacatl Battalion was American trained. You bought the massacre.

GIRL   What is the helicopter for?

BROADCASTER   Traffic report. Come in, come in. The Lieutenant Colonel in charge of the operation, Monterossa, was a vain man. He loved battle trophies. We allowed him to seize our transmitter once. When he went up in his helicopter to cart it home, we pressed a button —
(An explosion)
The wreckage of his machine is kept as a holy shrine where it fell from the sky that day.

GIRL   Where will you go?

BROADCASTER   Our station exploded into the static between stations.

We are the fourteen stations of the cross. The fourteen stations of Rufina Amaya's testimony; fourteen.

(A group enters and enacts a set of fourteen gestures, one per each of the fourteen previous scenes. The GIRL *is a full participant.)*

CHORUS
My heart is radio crystal
In my heart is the Thistle

(Old men and women bring roses to spots on the stage that are very particular to them, often leaving a picture or a token by the flower. They pray. The radio set is struck. When the gestures are complete.)

GIRL   Who are you?

BROADCASTER   I am Rose. Saint Rose of Lima. You have seen me before and you will see me again. I have endured every thorn. I live. I live in station Venceremos, the stations of the cross, my love crucified on static, stretched over the ice of all your skies. The crown of radio light is a crown of thorns.

GIRL   This was a Protestant region. The killings were political, not religious. Why —

BROADCASTER   The story must be told by means of every truth there is. Radio plays through you, my one. You tell.

GIRL   When they were killing the children, they threw the loud ones down a well. The children filled a *deep* well. The children are in the aquifer. Although you cannot hear them, their blood comes up roses; the blood of 75,000 martyrs rises, every weed a rose. I awake with a fist's worth of dirt from El Mozote in my pocket, now bright red. *(She pulls dirt from her pocket and scatters it.)*

CHORUS
Among these roses, during the day
The martyrs rise from the clay
Among these roses, through the night

Martyred bones rattle, combine
Among these roses, thorns of memory
Add my blood to theirs, this ground is holy

Who is to say
What happened here?

For the dead a rose
The dead arose
To say this is what happened here

For the dead a rose
The dead arose
To say this is what happened here

LOCUS

(John the Baptist)

Characters

SALOME

JOHN

SLEEPY LABEEF

ELVIS

BUDDY HOLLY

HEROD

HERODIAS

FIRST MAN

WAITRESS

JIM THORPE

NATHAN

MOTHER

WOLF

Locus was last performed by the Undermain Theatre at Addison Theatre–Stone Cottage, June 1994, as a part of Dallas's Chimera Festival, directed by Ivan Klousia. Artistic directors: Raphael Parry, Katherine Owens. Cast: Laurel Hoitsma, Raphael Parry, Ted Davey, David Lugo, Bruce Dubose, Rhonda Boutte, Tony Estrada, Routh Chadwick, Geronimo. Production: Mark Davies, Stephen Willis. Music: Nick Brisco.

Scene One: Husk

(Into a cramped mobile home high in the Albuquerque hills, red light filters down from the sky and up from the land. Behind and above, a small white plane flies. The red sun, held in the hands of a gray cloud, is halfway to the horizon, and dropping quickly. Buddy Holly's pained song, "Love Me," plays. The plane's engines start to whine; it becomes apparent that there's a crash in the making. The plane and sun are going to cross paths. They do cross paths. The engine sounds stop, the music stops, there's a loud snap, and the plane flies on in silence. The sun turns around and reveals Buddy's smiling head. The head sets and the moon rises. A wolf jumps up from the horizon; its jaws open nearly wide enough to split its head in two. The wolf holds the moon in its teeth. The stars are burrs caught in the wolf's coat. JOHN THE BAPTIST *sits on the edge of the bed in the mobile home, staring and dusty. He wears his belt knotted below the loops of his pants. He hears a cicada down by the pipes under the sink. He reaches towards it, carefully. He's about to grab it, when Salome bursts in;* JOHN *returns to the bed. Hebrew versions of Holly's songs play on the radio.)*

SALOME   Okay, you can start now. *(She crosses to a closet and starts rummaging.)*

JOHN   Stay out of that closet.

SALOME   You waste my time.

JOHN   Don't go.

SALOME   I've outgrown looking for arrowheads, but I just spent six hours looking for arrowheads so I could calm down enough to hear you say that. And it didn't work. I'm not calm. *(She continues to look through the closet.)*

JOHN   Don't go. Don't. *(She pulls out an outfit.)* Majorette? There's going to be some kind of dance involved? It was going to be a poem. You were going to do a poem.

SALOME   Couldn't make one up. It's going to be a dance. He likes dances.

JOHN   He wants me dead.

SALOME   He doesn't make mistakes like that. You think all he makes is mistakes.

JOHN   Don't dance at your daddy's birthday party.

SALOME   Quit talking about my daddy, please. Please.

JOHN   I don't even know if I'm here. Sure don't feel like Palestine. I got prophet-head. Can't stay in a time-frame.

SALOME   All that pollen in your clothes, you'd get honey in your shoes if you snapped a crease.

JOHN   You could make a poem if you want.

SALOME   You were so close to dead out there, why didn't you go all the way over?

JOHN   I wanted to look in on your daddy's little girl.

SALOME   You did what you came to do. Everybody got all hepped up about a whole untouchable cycle of paradoxes, and you been a baptizing fool. Baptized that one big fellow who's still living with his mother and blowing the miters on expensive cherry wood frames with a back saw he doesn't know how to sharpen in the only shop in town that'll have him, his dad's. Now you've got to stir this old thing up too. It's over. Where do you find water in a desert to baptize with, anyway?

JOHN   It's not about what you think.

SALOME   Herod marries Herodias. Names too close, for one thing. Then too she's one brother's niece, and another brother's wife, and I'm a daughter with five species of relationship to my parents and who cares because there it is. *(She changes into her costume.)*

JOHN   That's not the problem. That's what people latch onto. But it's more about his whole desire to pull everything into him and pull nothing out. The kinship business, that's the tip of the iceberg, that's nothing. Go ahead and dance, if you want to. But don't dance his way. For him. It's embarrassing. At least dance your way.

SALOME   It's going to be like a movie theater. I got it all worked out. Literally. You don't even have enough flesh on your face to pucker, do you?

JOHN   Stay here.

SALOME   I'm supposed to listen to another daddy?

JOHN   I see things. Desert things.

SALOME   You want to see how I'm going to dance?

JOHN   I want to tell you about the dreams I've been having. Wait just a little while. All I can think about is the end of things, when that's the opposite of what I want. Maybe I tell them to you and you can turn it around. Your going off to this party is an end of things, and maybe we can change that too. Listen.

SALOME   What kind of dreams?

JOHN   Names I can hardly pronounce. Geography I don't know.

SALOME   The wolf is swallowing the moon, babe. You have no time.

JOHN   The first is about a man climbing up a hill. *(Downstage, a Native American crosses to a lake and drinks like a deer. A MAN comes up behind him.)*

FIRST MAN   Thirsty?

JIM   Yeah.

FIRST MAN   From around here?

JIM   Yeah. Just got back.

FIRST MAN   Off the bus?

JIM   Yeah, I'll be going.

FIRST MAN   I'm very happy for you.

JIM   Why's that?

FIRST MAN   You're Thorpe? Jim Thorpe? All American?

JIM   Who are you?

FIRST MAN   You know.

JIM   What do you want?

FIRST MAN   You have the medals? You have the medals on you?

JIM   What about it? Just got back. *(A SECOND MAN enters.)*

SECOND MAN   Jim? Jim Thorpe?

JIM   Yeah?

FIRST MAN   Validation Committee. *(The SECOND MAN pulls a bat from behind his back and whacks JIM on the head, knocking him to the ground. The two men reach into JIM's kit bag and take his medals.)*

SECOND MAN   It's that semi-pro ball. You know, in your youth.

JIM   I made maybe fifty bucks. Fifty bucks total.

FIRST MAN   Go home. *(The two men leave.)*

JOHN   I have this picture though, that I should tell you about, of me losing my head in dying, when he gets tired of the things I say about him. At the same moment in spiritual time as I make my neck long for the sword, a man named Nathan in a diner in Arizona says: *(Nathan enters and sits at a diner counter. A* WAITRESS *joins him.)*

NATHAN   Two eggs over, toast, coffee.

WAITRESS   White toast?

NATHAN   Wheat. My wife is working bad medicine on me through white toast.

WAITRESS   Where's Jim?

NATHAN   He's not eating.

WAITRESS   He okay?

NATHAN   He says he found a spring on the mesa. He's climbing up there now.

WAITRESS   You need breakfast to climb up a hill.

NATHAN   He's looking for his spirit guide again.

WAITRESS   He's an old man. He can do whatever he wants.

NATHAN   Older every time he goes up. *(*JIM *ages as he walks, and he follows a stream uphill.)*

JOHN   Skinny as winter in summer, walking tilted, laughing. Busted teeth, arms angled like Mr. Peanut. At a standstill.

NATHAN   I made him salami sandwiches but he feeds them to the reptiles. He's the master of his tongue and belly. He gives it all away.

JOHN   Hung as a jewel on the throat of the mountain.

JIM   The silver hands of the stream make sign language for "water" over and over. The red bottom of the stream is the hidden message behind the sign. *(The* WAITRESS *enters wearing a bear's head; she stands before* JIM.*)*

SALOME   No bears on the mesa.

JOHN   No stream either.

NATHAN *(Standing)*   The spirit guide stands in front of him. A bear — it plucks up a trout, which is the hand of the river. Abrupt and stiff. As tensely mortal as any miracle. The fish points to the top of the mesa, and Jim climbs in the wind. Blistered in the nicotine sand. *(The bear eats the fish, and* NATHAN *exits hand in hand with the bear.)*

JIM   I see red in the stream and I see my life flowing away. Because of power plant pollution? Because of a corruption in the land? I think, no, I think because water flows downhill, and I am red, and gold is mine. My water, red, and gold medals flow down into the ground; I see, and go up. Because: a waitress in a bear's head holds trout-in-air, saying: "your head is nowhere in this world — the head is impossible. Go away to the source of the stream and the belly button of loss." I stand simultaneous with the moment of all my loss. Look how old I am! And I am so sad. And I am not afraid. And I become something else. *(He raises his arms, for flight. We hear the wind gather behind him.)* I eat no breakfast in the city these days. I eat no food at all. The world wishes me elsewhere. And I live over the ground, I die like a fish, I die in air, because I live not on the ground but in the wish of the world. There is no justice here. *(He is knocked face forward by the wind. Pause, and he exits.)*

JOHN   At the same moment as my head is chopped into the air, Jim Thorpe is cut by wind-sword from the mesa. Kissed to oblivion by a breeze. Everything is sliced from Jim, and death streams through his head. From this dream I know that there is a gap to elsewhere through hunger in wind.

SALOME *(Fascinated. Scared. Not won over)*   They're waiting for me. Daddy's birthday.

JOHN   Not yet. You go, and I die. The more I talk about it, the more I know it. One more desert thing.

SALOME   Okay. One. *(BUDDY HOLLY and his mother sit at a kitchen table. The MOTHER looks out the window and BUDDY reads a paper.)*

MOTHER   What's good, Buddy?

BUDDY   Right here. State. State fair. *(He shows his MOTHER the write-up.)*

MOTHER   World's largest watermelon.

BUDDY   No. Look who's playing.

MOTHER   Sleepy LaBeef? Elvis Presley?

BUDDY   Patsy Montana!

JOHN   His mother goes to see the watermelon and Buddy Holly goes to hear Patsy Montana. But they stick around for the whole show because they have microphones and the sound is pretty good. Elvis almost doesn't make it on. He busted his guitar strings in rehearsal, and he's almost crying, and Sleepy LaBeef comes through with a loaner. *(A young and not corny ELVIS enters and holds BUDDY's head between his hands. He speaks evenly, without inflection, and BUDDY repeats.)*

ELVIS   Train arrive —

BUDDY   Train arrive —

ELVIS   Sixteen coaches long —

BUDDY   Sixteen coaches long —

ELVIS   Well that long black train —

BUDDY   Well that long black train —

ELVIS   Got my baby and gone.

BUDDY   Got my baby and gone. *(*ELVIS *and* BUDDY *stand apart from one another, teaching each other moves in slow motion. Down stage,* SLEEPY LABEEF *gives a radio interview.)*

SLEEPY   Patsy Montana headlining. I was next, and this ridiculous looking kid, I mean I thought so at the time, come up the steps while I was coming off. And tears were shaking loose all around him. I couldn't understand him at first. But it got to where I figured he needed to borrow a guitar, so I gave him mine. He didn't want a strap — that had my name on it — I thought then maybe he's sit down and play some mid-tempo song about amusing mules. But he gets up there and screws himself around trying to hold that guitar up with one leg. Some of the guys are laughing, but a couple of the girls are squealing high, like at a dog in a window. The more he works himself into a knot, trying to stop crying and make that alien guitar subject to the might of his fists, the more the crowd is stirred by the touch of private hands. Elvis really bears down now. He's got through about a song and a half barely singing, just half sobbing, half in a forceful dream. So he chokes the life out of the guitar neck and wham — breaks five strings in a chord. It was a C chord, as I recall. Now I had played all my life and had broken maybe one string once. *(*BUDDY *and* ELVIS *sing a slow, a cappella "Heartbeat.")* The way I figure it, I didn't break strings because the strings hand already been broken inside me. There was nobody or nothing strong enough to break the strings in Elvis, he was that fierce a guitar. He tried to get Jesus and the martial arts to break them, but they couldn't do it. Some men get their strings broke and never get a hit. Some men die trying to break the strings. *(*BUDDY, ELVIS *and* SLEEPY *exit.)*

JOHN   At the same moment: my head with its last electric conclusion, Jim Thorpe, and Buddy's powerful plane are all in the air. I see my heroes. I see my heroes and they are blown away. And through these pictures I also get that you must broadcast what you now. It's been centuries, Salome. I been dead so long, and nothing in my head is in my time. There should be justice, and there is a future, and I must broadcast. I will not know the justice, or the future, or the signal reception while I'm a living thing. But there you go. Prophet head. Cicada shell. *(He looks around and sees* SALOME *has backed out onto the road.)* Salome? It's not fair of you to take advantage of me when I'm seeing things.

SALOME   I don't want to hear all about the end of things.

JOHN   But I got to tell you.

SALOME   If you're after justice, It's my daddy who brings the hammer down. And if you're after broadcast, I can tune you out. And if you're broadcasting justice, John, then you're down and out.

JOHN   Well, I know that too. I want to put a drop of water on your head, so you can feel it run down.

SALOME   I don't want to hear all about the end of things, John the Baptist!

Scene Two: Crushed Red Velvet

*(*SALOME, *wearing her special cheerleader clothes, stands in the bed of a pick-up truck. A red velvet curtain is drawn across the inside of the rear window.)*

SALOME   Like a movie, Daddy. Go! *(The curtain goes up. Loews-wise.* HEROD *and* HERODIAS *kneel on the seat, and they're the audience.* SALOME *puts an ancient version of a Sousa march on a cardboard record player, and dances a pattern. It is not a comfortable sight.* SALOME *is eager to please, but she's not dancing her dance. She finishes with a split.)* The end. *(Applause)* What do I get, Herod?

HEROD *(Through speakers, like at a drive-up fast food window)* Half my kingdom and all that's in it?

HERODIAS   Go ahead, honey, ask him.

SALOME   I want the head of John the Baptist. On a nice silver platter, please.

Scene Three: Bait

(HEROD's bar-b-q. HEROD is a kind of devil over the sawed-in-half oil drum grill; his face is red from the heat, and his cooking fork is huge. All the food is either bright red or bright yellow: corn, steak, lobster. SA-LOME sits to one side, in the dirt, leashed with rope to a spike in the ground. She's bait. JOHN sneaks towards the bait, and everyone pretends not to notice. HEROD and HERODIAS tell each other a story.)

HEROD   He did his broken knee walk from the trailer up the red clay scrabble of the ancient, beat to shit arrowhead hills. Peeping up over at our camp, where the plastic lanterns were beginning to brighten in the dusk. The pattern was as at a carnival. Yellows and reds, corn and meat, chili con carnival.

JOHN   They're always leaving babies out.

HEROD   He can't resist the most precious head of the girl. The one he is compelled to baptize; compelled by dryness to find water, compelled by water to find the source, compelled by the source to find the other place. But my place is the place for my daughter. She is staked out; a rope knotted to a looped re-bar driven deep into the ground. She is on her leash in the clearing, and he peeps. She's the white crow. She's bait.

SALOME   She almost warns him. *(JOHN approaches. He doesn't make eye-contact; he moves as if he were approaching a wounded wolf.)*

JOHN   Don't don't don't. Nothing. Sh. Nothing to it.

HERODIAS   Herod's sword is the moment in time.

JOHN   You know, when I reach my hand out, I find water. *(He reaches behind.)*

HEROD   He is nabbed in the act of reaching. *(*JOHN *is grabbed and brought before* HEROD, *who suddenly speaks fake Oklahoman.)*

HEROD   Welcome to our picnic, John.

HERODIAS   Yes, John, yes.

HEROD   Are you hungry?

HERODIAS   Are you hungry, yes?

HEROD   You don't eat.

HERODIAS   Eat, eat.

HEROD   Before you die, John —

HERODIAS   Yes, before you die —

HEROD   There's one question.

HERODIAS   We've been wondering.

HEROD   Who baptizes *you?* I mean, how does that happen, if you're the baptism king? You know, I'm handy that way too.

HERODIAS   Yes.

HEROD   Yes, I have a talent in that area. I baptize thee, in the name of all that's mine. *(He nods, and his henchmen dunk* JOHN's *head into the boiling corn-water. Dusk. When* JOHN's *horrid face is yanked shocked from the wicked water, light collects around him and around* SALOME.)

SALOME   When the day is over and darkness comes, John's blind head is pulled from the corn-water, squiggling like a balloon let go as his last breath escapes him. The lanterns are ripening bright; one sways over John, and one sways over Salome, who is pinned to the stake. John remembers Salome. *(HEROD draws a chef's knife to decapitate JOHN, and the blade flashes in the dark. Lights off SALOME.)*

JOHN   The headless body will hunt the head. This ceaseless head, this desire to dance, this wind knocked man. This trout in air in the hand of the bear, this wreck, this water. This daughter. This daughter. *(Last light fades from JOHN's flying head.)*

PAIN
(Eulalia)

Characters

EULALIA

MAGGIE

DAD

BODY OF LIZ

Pain was first produced at BACA in Brooklyn in March 1991, as part of the series' premiere, directed by Jennifer McDowall. Artistic director: Bonnie Metzger. Other series directors: Fritz Ertl, Thalia Field, Brian Mertes, Bonnie Metzger, and Randolyn Zinn. Cast: Alison Fleminger, Cheryl Rogers, Glen Santiago, Julia Martin. Production: Chris Doyle, Barbara Cohig, Betsy Finston, David Woolard, Marilyn Zalkan, Chuck Streeper, Marvin Gentile, Amanda Junquera, Kyle Chepulis, Stephen Kellam, Dawn Groenewegen.

Scene One: Panorama

(Dark. DAD *comes on humming, tiptoeing.)*

DAD   Where's Miss Mouse? Where's my Mouse Knuckles? *(Lights on. The flayed and burned corpse of his daughter in among stuffed animals on the white lace coverlet of her bed. Lights off.)* Where's Miss Mouse? Where's Mouse Knuckles? *(Lights up. The corpse is gone. He calls off.)* Honey, we must have a word about Liz. I can't — I can't keep — Lights off, lights on. I could swear she was there. Face in the lamp shade. Body in the chair. Walk through these halls, lights off, lights on. Every shape in the shadows, tells me she's gone. Lights off, lights on, doesn't matter to me. Every flick of the switch dumps eternity. *(*MAGGIE *enters opposite.)*

MAGGIE   I'm going out looking.

DAD   Moonlight shadows of dew, electric shadows of stone. The shadow of your smile chills me to the bone.

MAGGIE   For where they have taken her.

DAD   Keep talking to me. *(Lights down and up.* MAGGIE *stands in a vertical rectangle of florescence, amid subway noises — she's riding the train, looking out the front.)*

MAGGIE   When you start talking in song lyrics — that's it. I go. Swept like pulse into the critter. He's trying to spell himself to me. F train, J, M, D, R, 9, 4, A. Pulse and stop. How did I get to Bush Terminal? Pulse and stop. How did I get to the Terminal Bar across the street from Van Cortland Park in the Bronx? Why am I drinking green beer? Back, pulse, and stop now at the Queens Museum where I meet the brutal boy. They have a panorama there, dear. Our city to scale, you look down on it. The salt marshes, East New York — the size of Europe, the graveyards, airports, top forty songs. My daughter taken away and sacrificed in the New York Corn Ceremony. The boy priest slips his hand in mine. *(A giant with all his veins exposed, wearing a ceremonial headdress made of corn husks, enters and holds* MAGGIE's *hand.)* He tells me the cult has taken her, but won't tell me where she is. *(To the priest.)* I am in the system. I am the avenging cell. I am towards your name, from inside. *(The priest leaves.)* I ride the subways all day long, babe. It is perfect there for about sixty seconds. On the Brooklyn bound F when it goes el at Smith and Ninth. I hear an approach, and am by now more than willing to kill anything that comes towards me. But it's a man playing a machine with his mouth. It's an old man with taped glasses playing a clarinet — "Shadow of Your Smile." Corny, and good, really good. Out the window, it's actually day time. One of the new Metrotech buildings downtown holds its red sun mouth open for evening's reed. Everywhere the funny red so prevalent in cartoons. We collapse utterly towards Seventh Avenue, and the man has to stop playing and collect because a lot of people get off here. My husband back home crying right into a Bugs Bunny cartoon. Liz watched cartoons. Where is the body of my daughter? Behind what cartoon, where on the staff have they hidden her? What true and clean image of suffering can sum me beyond the city's abominable final line? *(From left to right, an old man crosses, playing "Shadow of Your Smile" on clarinet. Fade out. Lights up on an old Spanish town.* MAGGIE *stands to one side of the stage.* EULALIA *enters, a girl of twelve. She addresses the audience.* MAGGIE *can't see her yet.)*

EULALIA *(What she says, shows.)*   In my home town, the judge is being shaved by a eunuch with the same blade that emasculated the former boy. The judge is that confident of his authority. The shaving soap runs in the gutter. Everywhere the streets are damp — they have been hosed down for the parade. The grown-ups are behind closed doors and shutters, protesting the ritual. But the young ones are drawn out when the militia scatters fruit on the ground. Seven-year-olds squat like monkeys and eat fruit the size of small heads, and their parents give up and stand over them, suspending age over the staring, quick, curled children, monkeys eating heads. The parade comes; a gross sugar cake piled on a bier honors the god of this judge's capital authority. *(The parade starts to pass. Blackout.)*

SUBWAY ANNOUNCER'S VOICE *(In the darkness)*   Fourth Century, everybody off. *(Lights up. The crowd is frozen.* MAGGIE *speaks to the man next to her.)*

MAGGIE   Stillwell? Stillwell Avenue?

MAN   You're in Merida, Spain. Today is the day Saint Eulalia is martyred. She's only twelve years old. That's her there. You want to go back home. You don't speak our language.

MAGGIE, EULALIA (MAGGIE *to the man*, EULALIA *to the Judge*)
    Where are they taking the cake?

MAN   Get back in your own story. *(He blinds and gags* MAGGIE.*)*

EULALIA   Wait!

MAN   She can't see you now. *(The parade continues and the crowd unfreezes. The* JUDGE *wipes his face with a towel and takes his place at the head of the procession.* EULALIA *walks backwards in front of him.)*

EULALIA   Where are they taking the cake?

JUDGE   For the priests to eat.

EULALIA   Which priests?

JUDGE   My priests. The razor priests.

EULALIA   Does the Emperor know about this?

JUDGE   He bought the sugar. Out of the way, Eulalia. *(*EULALIA *stands still and stops the parade.)* Diocletian forbids dissent. Forbids what you and your family practice.

EULALIA   My flesh is draining towards my bones, and pouring down the copper tubing of my legs. Everywhere I am carried down holes in this city.

JUDGE   I will give you a crisp new dollar bill if you go away.

EULALIA   The gold eaters, the cake wasters, the anorexic pagan priests have put a fuse into our filth.

JUDGE You are always such trouble, Eulalia. I will have to kill you, Eulalia.

EULALIA No no no no parade. *(She spits on the cake.)*

JUDGE If we cannot have cake, then we will have plain bread. *(The unfleshed boy priest enters and steals* EULALIA *away.* MAGGIE *moans loudly. Blackout)*

Scene Two: Martyrdom

DAD *(In the blackout)* What's that you say, honey? What's that you say? They plucked her flesh with fishhooks and she refused to renounce her faith? Who is this now? *(He is lit by the light of cartoons from a TV. He laughs low and steady; the lights come on.)* What's that you say, honey? What's that you say? They burned her alive in the bread ovens in Merida? And who would this be, Maggie? *(*MAGGIE *enters wrapped in a blanket. She sits by her husband.)*

MAGGIE No, no. I was saying when I first started running through the subway tunnels, on account of the lateness of the hour and the rarity of trains, I was saying that when I first started running mad and waving through the New York subway tunnels looking for our missing daughter — I was blind. My eyes weren't used to the dark, and all I could see was Eulalia's martyrdom. *(*EULALIA *wheels in on a gurney.)*

EULALIA *(To herself as much as anybody)* The first thing to catch fire is my hair, and it becomes so beautiful I cry. A China mountain full of birds and mist. Blades open holes in my skin and I press seeds in and the pain squirts like bean roots in wet tissue paper left on the window sill in bio class. Cool translucent growing pain. The tendons expand and contract. I sit up awfully and the crowd backs away from the oven's mouth. All things sealed blow open, like branches, likes dusk's woodwind mouth tightened on anger. I am, finally, a grin. *(*EULALIA *lies still.* MAGGIE *crosses and covers her with her blanket.* MAGGIE's *skin is flaky.)*

MAGGIE I was saying that the kidnap of our daughter has floured me with eczema. Running down the subway tunnels in the corn priest's system I am exhausted by the visions of Eulalia, and even though I have to wrap myself in a wet blanket to keep my skin from cracking to pieces, cracked as crusted bread, I take the blanket and cover the girl.

DAD   Who is this now?

MAGGIE   Eulalia and I have become plain bread. My eyes are used to the dark now. I have been everywhere, and I'm still running. My visions will come as they come, not recollected — but through a world that's become transparent to me. Mary appears in the horrible rock of Masabielle, in the World's Fair Ground in Queens. Eulalia in tunnels. My daughter then can appear to me in cartons. Transparent. *(Bugs Bunny plays on a large screen upstage — the "Tree Grows in Brooklyn" episode.* MAGGIE *addresses the audience.)* I found my daughter hanging from a tree in Prospect Park, sacrificed in the New York Corn Ceremony. When I knew she was missing I ran through the subway tunnels, station to station, when I was in a vision where she was. Here is my daughter. *(She walks, clutches her stomach, stands, reaches, walks, clutches.)* I want Liz. I want Liz. I want Liz. *(*DAD *and* EULALIA *clear.)*

Scene Three: Hell and Glory

(A tree in Prospect Park. EULALIA *and* LIZ *hang side by side stripped of skin. A man with the head of Porky Pig, naked from the waist down, large genitals poking out between the tails of his shirt, a bloody pruning hook in one hand and the skins in the other, stands and listens to the two girls sing.)*

LIZ, EULALIA
  In the central field by the lake in the park
  I am hung upon a tree by bandits in the dark
  A snipped vocal chord in the throat of a lark
  Yields a speaking bird singing words, singing words

  Naked in March on a bare limbed tree
  The miraculous bird sings a prayer over me

My bare skin sore with the blood of gravity
The mutilated bird singing words, singing words

My spirit springs up
From the neutral singing tree
Late march snow
Blesses bodies left back
Gravity's surd, the singing snipped bird
Is benediction's sick trigger, is the last word heard

(A gunshot, but not from the pig. The heads of the girls hang limp, and the pig exits. Two Merida musicians enter.)

FIRST MUSICIAN   It doesn't snow in Merida.

SECOND MUSICIAN   Take Eulalia back. *(They wrap* EULALIA *in white cloth, taking her down from the tree.)* For decency's sake. *(*DAD *and* MAGGIE *enter.* MAGGIE *sees her daughter,* DAD *doesn't.)*

DAD   Honey, where are you going? Your face is changing. You're in another dimension. *(*MAGGIE *climbs the tree and hangs from* EULALIA's *spike.)*

MAGGIE   I found her hung a yard off Hell's floor, the subway breathing against her legs. Burnt, made one and perfect by the snow. Annulled from the city. The corn ceremony forgotten in the enduring perfection of her image in my head. I heard her singing with St. Eulalia. A kind of bitterness in it, but finally abandoning me. Bloom in the fire, sing, expire. I came to the park, dear, to learn how to be snow-buried after burning. This is the perilous circle. Guarded by burning bushes. You can't enter here. I found my daughter hung from a tree in Prospect Park. *(She hangs in silence, and her husband looks on, sitting cross-legged on the ground. A circle of fire separates him from the tree. Blackout)*

POLIO COMES FROM THE MOON

(Bernadette)

Characters

BERNADETTE

MARY

MOTHER

MAILLE

BERCEUSE

OTHER SISTERS

LIANNE

Polio Comes from the Moon is unproduced. It was first published in *Performing Arts Journal* 44 (May 1993).

(BERNADETTE gathers sticks by the river. MARY Mother of God appears behind her.)

MARY   Bernadette? *(BERNADETTE sees her. MARY sings.)*
Interrogate the landscape
Reveal, reveal me
Take my colors from the snow and sky
Stars from the sky
My girl, reveal me

I will whisper secrets of
Immaculate Conception
And the Virgin Birth
But first
Scrape the Earth
Scrape the Earth
Scrape the Earth

See what your Mother Mary brings
In the middle of winter
Life springs
I bring a spring
Scrape the Earth

(BERNADETTE does. A spring flows.)

BERNADETTE   A spring! *(MARY exits. BERNADETTE'S MOTHER and five SISTERS enter; a later time and a further place.)*

MOTHER   Bring her back

MAILLE   She says she has another mother now.

MOTHER   I'm her mother, Maille, and yours too. She's been out there long enough. And she's lost her mind. Bring her back. *(MAILLE and her SISTERS set out.)*

SISTERS
> The sixth sister missed her mother's cry to come home
> She always gleaned the shore for what the river gave
> Five sisters missed her and they searched her in the eddy's foam
> The noon sun comes and the water starts to rave

> What the river gave
> Windfall kindling
> A girl up to the cave
> Mother Mary's darling

> Bernadette rests on her knees, breathes shallowly
> Listens carefully on the banks of the Gave
> A girl of fourteen speaks low and naturally
> Bernadette's guest on Masabielle

(The SISTERS *draw near;* MAILLE *crosses to* BERNADETTE.*)*

MAILLE   I don't see Mary.

BERNADETTE   I do.

MAILLE   I don't. Some people believe you. They say there have been cures.

BERNADETTE   There have been.

MAILLE   When will you come home?

BERNADETTE   Why are you so sad? *(*MAILLE *rejoins her other* SISTERS.*)*

MAILLE
> Where our sister goes all knowledge ends
> And school will no more serve her
> Suspended in the shattered rock
> Aureole of water

> The flashing of the secret sign
> I believe she sees her

Bernadette is not the same
Eighteen visions later

OTHER SISTERS
    Maille we won't go home
    Won't go home without her
    Maille, save her, save us all
    We don't believe she sees her

MAILLE   I looked into her eyes. What comes to Lourdes comes through her. What she says is true.

OTHER SISTERS   Then we should stay with her.

MAILLE   We will. She has visions but they don't make her happy. They tucker her out. She has *eighteen* visions. (MARY *visits with* BERNADETTE.)

MARY
    First, signs
    Sign's a concept
    First, conceive

    Then, the world
    Then a babe
    Then believe

    Then, the actions
    Childhood, more
    Then consent to being

    The many figures
    And forms taken on: the
    Ideals' publicity
    Ways to know knowing

    Eighteen visions
    Eighteen visions of heaven

    Seventeen droughts
    And seventeen floods

The world is deep, the world is wide
Seventeen rivers band the land
My son died

The child of this day breaks the plates the Earth bakes
I do no promise to make you happy
In this world, but the next
Where vision eighteen wakes
You up

MAILLE   What comes to Lourdes comes through her, but what leaves
through Lourdes leaves through me. I have *my* visions. First, our sister
will die at the age of thirty-six, in a town we've never been to. Mean-
while, in Korea, a girl is being eaten by the moon.
  Late in the next century
  A girl comes here from Asia
  The moon is eating both her legs
  In the mountains of Korea
She will leave Lourdes as she came. I do not know what this means yet.

(LIANNE *enters in a wheelchair. She sees only* MAILLE, *and* MAILLE
alone sees her.)

LIANNE, MAILLE
  Polio comes from the moon
  On gray-green bee wings
  Settling on red petals
  An ash unseen

  Through limitless space
  A bit of polio
  The flower lifts its face
  Flowers are made so

  The moon-faced lavender-lashed polio king
  Smokes his garden hives, bee releasing
  Ash snow drifts and flowers swoon
  I believe polio comes from the moon

Buzzing little bee
Of moonlight's making
Bee, release me
My legs are breaking

Polio sleeps with my legs on the moon
Polio sleeps with me
Polio sleeps in my nectar in me
Polio sleeps with me

(MAILLE *and the other* SISTERS *join* BERNADETTE.)

BERCEUSE   Bernadette, we'll stay, but I am troubled by —

BERNADETTE   Sh, Berceuse.

BERCEUSE   We are wondering — is the Korean girl Maille sees the agent
of your death?

MAILLE   Does she —

MOTHER *(Offstage)*   Bernadette! (BERNADETTE *rises and holds*
MARY's *hand.)*

BERNADETTE
   I see her. Leave me alone
   I'm snagged in the hand of the hill this winter
   God has caught a splinter

   Leave me alone. I see her
   How can I tell you what I see?
   I must get her words exactly

She says
Know and build, she says
Know your sins and pray
The words are hers
The mouth is mine
We speak in left hand, right hand

Mother of Facts
Know and build
I see the Virgin every day

MARY *(To* BERNADETTE*)*   Listen to your sister.

BERNADETTE   To you. Tell me which ones will—

BERCEUSE *(To* MAILLE*)*   What is the other girl doing now?

MAILLE   Lianne. Her name is Lianne.

BERCEUSE   What is Lianne doing?

LIANNE
Routes of trade and travel
Branches on a tree
Westward cities:
Leaves

All the strange ports of call
The mountains and the rivers all
Fall into the sacred waters
Where the Virgin pleads for me

My bundle of afflictions
Up against the massed petitions
Is as small as rain that falls across
The Occident Gulf and the African Sea

MAILLE   She's on her way here.

BERNADETTE   Which ones will get better?

MARY   Listen to your sister. You and Maille split the eighteenth vision.

BERNADETTE   You're gone.

MARY   Yes.

BERNADETTE   Since you started coming, there have been crowds. Everybody wants to see the queen. To get well. What do I say? Lady, I can't stay here without you.

MARY   Goodbye. *(She exits.* BERCEUSE *comes up on* BERNADETTE, *startling her.)*

BERCEUSE   You don't have to come home. We'll take care of things. We'll build a chapel and mind it.

MAILLE *(Also to* BERNADETTE.*)*   I see you gone. Gone to die young.

BERNADETTE

Sisters of Notre Dame, Notre Dame at Nevers
Never return to Lourdes. It's the day to day forever

I admire Alphonsus Rodriguez standing at the door
Saint of the day to day. I can't see her anymore

I can't see the blessed mother, won't spy on one more hopeful face
Waiting on a miracle in this haunted granite place

Leave me alone at Nevers in Notre Dame sisterhood
I've got chores to do. Goodbye
I saw what I could
Gather wood

It is no gift
To see and believe
I have to leave
It's not my place
To see and endure
There is no cure

One in a million
Walks away
Now go away

One in a million
Walks again

This is the end
The end
(*Speaking*) She left me. (BERNADETTE *leaves Lourdes for Nevers.*)

MAILLE
Come back
Come back Bernadette
Mamma says it's all right
If you want to stay late

Come back baby
Come back

27,000 gallons of water a week
27,000 visitors
A rapids of pilgrims
27,000

Come back to Lourdes, Bernadette
Our hands are cold and losing their fists
We're waiting, waiting
In the hall of the Mountain Queen

If you come back now
If you come back to me
I won't say a word.
(BERNADETTE *crosses to* MAILLE *and draws her aside.*)

BERNADETTE   I can only come back this way.

MAILLE   Your body's not here.

BERNADETTE   Don't scare the others. They've been through enough.
We do the last vision together. The girl. Lianne. She's up at the shrine.

LIANNE   Up the stone hill. Under my own power. Many hundreds
around me. Into the cool cave. In the cave, so few around me. The at-
tending nuns take me into a room for women, and change me into the
robes they provide. They walk me down into the shallow pool, towards

the source, towards Mary's fountainhead. I feel nothing on my legs, of course, but at my waist, the temperature pleases me.

BERNADETTE   I'm sorry, Lianne.

LIANNE   They are praying and praying, touching me, where I can't feel. I don't know what to make of the praying, but the water is fine — new — even after so many millions through.

MAILLE   You are taken back out.

BERNADETTE   No cures at all that day.

MAILLE   One in a million walks.

BERNADETTE
    Hail Mary of thee I sing
    I wait for your answer
    Nothing nothing
    Transparent air in search of seeming
    Mother of Facts I am
    Waiting waiting
    Nothing nothing

    This one for example, the grotto breaks her
    She's scrap of meat hung in the teeth of Nature

    Accept, please, my rude apology
    The moon's mad hunger for the sea tonight

    The water steals a blanket from the stars
    Dark walks a cold kitchen and boils up a pot of light

    Final tide, and rude apology
    They take her out, cradled arms
    I see through these spectacles

    No you show nothing
    No miracle
    No you show me nothing new

(Speaking, to MAILLE.*)* The polio doesn't come from the moon — what that part means is that the moon wakes hope. It does in lovers. It lifts hope like a wave. But hope and waves can't reach the moon for wishing.

MAILLE   Lianne isn't finished yet.

LIANNE
    True faith is not found at Lourdes
    Wonders turned in the way of tender mercies
    True faith is not found on pilgrimage
    Prayer's hoe works furrows in the rosary rain

    Mother Mary has no time for that
    Bernadette likewise refuses return
    Faith won't fit in an age of time
    Action burns. True faith is sacrificial

    True faith lies in leaving Lourdes
    Like a spring, faith is always moving
    Leave Lourdes like water

    True faith lies in leaving Lourdes
    The cures, the lures of time and time
    True faith lies in leaving Lourdes
    True faith lies in leaving Lourdes
    True faith lies in leaving Lourdes

*(*LIANNE *speaks to* MAILLE *and Bernadette directly.)* One in a million walks away. But a million walks in a new way. It is nothing to see and believe. The heroes of Lourdes are the ones who are strong enough to leave the hillside at all, before any promise has been fulfilled, or even made. This world and its signs are nothing, are obscure and misleading, unless you look with the eyes of faith, first. *(She exits.)*

MAILLE *(To* BERNADETTE.*)*   You're gone. You are young and gone, now.

BERNADETTE   Yes. *(*BERNADETTE *exits. The other* SISTERS *run on.)*

BERCEUSE   You found her?

OTHER SISTERS   Will she come back?

MAILLE   It's daytime?

BERCEUSE   Yes.

MAILLE   And the moon is still in the sky?

BERCEUSE   Yes.

MAILLE   It was night when I began combat. I saw the moon's pupil adjust on me, and I was held safe in vision. The moon halved, quartered; the eye shut. I do not know where Bernadette is. The moon comes out in the daytime sometimes. She has a vision of me, sees me now as she sees Mary. Sees us all, day, night. Lord have mercy on her. Lord have mercy on me. Lord have mercy on the third eye. We return now to sweep the chapel. *(They sweep, and sing two Hail Mary's.* BERNADETTE *lends her voice; she wears a wedding veil, being married now to God in heaven.)*

TREE OF HOPE, KEEP FIRM

(Mary, the Annunciation)

Characters

VIRGIN MARY

YOUNG MARY

ANNE

GABRIEL

JOSEPH

FACILITATORS (the FACILITATORS speak some of the
stage directions and control the mise en scène)

Tree of Hope, Keep Firm was first performed at Intersection for the Arts in San Francisco, April 1993, directed by the playwright. Codirector: Cianna Stewart. Artistic director and producer: Paul Codiga. Cast: Denise Cavaliere, Jennifer Bainbridge, Sammie Choy, Troy Anthony Harris, Robert Molossi, Johnna Marie Schmidt, David Todd. Production: Douglas Holmes, Colin Hale, Brook Stanton, Nina Siegal. Live Music: Edith Rules (Derek Cheever, Leslie Jackson, Alan Whitman).

Title from Frida Kahlo.

(A YOUNG MARY *and her mother sit in a tower window.* ANNE *is teaching* MARY *how to read, but* MARY *is distracted, looking out the window. In the field below are seven clay incarnations of the adult Mary: The Sacred Heart, the Pieta, in Ascension, as Queen of Saints, Kneeling at the Cross, By the Manger, Riding the Donkey. An eighth, live Mary, hides in the lake, trembling, wet.* ANNE *turns the* YOUNG MARY*'s head back to the book.)*

ANNE   Put the letters together. Sound it out.

YOUNG MARY   Behold, a Virgin shall be with child, and shall bring forth a son, and shall call his name — *(Struggling with a word)*

ANNE   Emanuel.

YOUNG MARY   Emanuel, which, being interpreted is, God with us. *(The sound of beating wings. A boy angel enters and spreads broad wings. He looks among the clay Marys and then turns to the Mary in the lake.* YOUNG MARY *sees this, and breaks away from* ANNE.)

ANNE   Wait! *(Lights out in the tower and* ANNE *exits. The* YOUNG MARY *runs to the elder.)*

MARY   Mary my hope.

YOUNG MARY   You're going to be taken.

MARY   We've been found. That's all he needs.

YOUNG MARY   Don't listen.

MARY   We're listening already.

YOUNG MARY   Then say something to him. *(*MARY *rises from the lake.)*

MARY   There's more time than you think. It takes a long time to listen. I'm going to get drunk tonight. See if I don't. Get me some clothes. Not my mother's — not *our* mother's. Some stranger's. We'll put them back on the line in the morning. *(*YOUNG MARY *exits.* MARY *dances with* GABRIEL; *lively.)*

I am your maiden
Hand maiden
Maiden of God
I live to serve

I am your sword
You've drawn the sword
I live to serve
See if I don't

I am your bride
The virgin bride
Tonight will be
The bride's night

I want to know where the money goes
I want to see my suffering
I want to go where I can think
In a corset of plaster
Orchard of bone

*(*GABRIEL *backs out.* YOUNG MARY *enters with clothes.* MARY *begins to change.* GABRIEL *returns as a young boy, driving ducks to the lake.)* Close the curtains. *(*YOUNG MARY *draws curtains painted with a dense forest scene suggestive of internal human anatomy. We see* MARY's *silhouette through this.* GABRIEL *stands and watches. He tries to get a duck to talk.)*

GABRIEL   Go over there and say something. Hey. Like this. *(He moves his mouth carefully.)* Say words like I'm saying now. Say "Emanuel." "God with us." Tell her something bigger than her or me. Tell her I'm Gabriel, and I've taken a ruler to the night and can give her the final number. *(The silhouette disappears.)* She's going away! Emanuel! God with us! *(The curtains open. Tableau.* MARY *is gone, and in her place, a fawn shot with arrows. The fawn has the head of the* YOUNG MARY. *The boy tries to stay calm.)* I haven't come to see you. I've come to break the silence. With the other Mary.

YOUNG MARY   I am full of arrows. Flint points hunt their knowledge in me. I am what the arrows need to know. I am persuasive of stone-in-air. I am still. Therefore smarter than the woods.

GABRIEL   My ducks and I will retire to the cottage for the evening. *(He exits. The fawn runs off.* MARY *enters in a beautiful dress; she holds* YOUNG MARY's *hand.)*

MARY   Everything's alcohol when it's this humid and it's summer, but there's a breeze and you've got the right dress. The kind of alcohol that protects your brain in a cushion of music.

YOUNG MARY   Don't say anything you'll regret.

MARY   He's less than me. He has no ideas. *(Lightning falls into the lake, and sticks there. A delicate electrical sound.* YOUNG MARY *and* MARY *dance.)*

MARY/YOUNG MARY
     I will get drunk tonight
     See if I don't
     Lightning jumps from the sun tonight
     See if I don't

     I will turn the suitor back tonight
     See if I don't
     The moon outshines the sun tonight
     See if I don't

*(*YOUNG MARY *stumbles.* MARY *picks her up; the girl notices* MARY's *scars.)*

YOUNG MARY   You have nine wounds! Where will I get those?

MARY   Only one. Feels like nine. *(The pieces of lightning assemble to form a skeleton with the head of a hungry wolf.* MARY *continues.)* We will not know death tonight. Life and death seek us fiercely. But you see? The wolf is blind. The eyes look off in crazy directions. *(The wolf comes forward, tanglefoot. It starts to rain.)* It's starting to rain. Don't worry. *(MARY holds her younger self in her arms, sprouts wings, and flies around the stage. It takes four people to operate MARY's wings. The wolf pursues, hits a wall, shatters, and disappears. The MARYS run under a tree. We see the tree above and below the ground: complicated roots and breaking, ripe fruit. MARY notices drops of red on her white blouse.)* The rain's opened the fruit. Climb up. *(YOUNG MARY climbs the tree. She's surprised by the boy angel's winged head, which flies into the tree beside her. He has a third eye in the middle of his forehead, and the lids move like lips.)*

GABRIEL *(To MARY)*   Hail, thou that art highly favored. *(A panel in the roots slides away. The tap roots wind around a fetal Jesus.)*

YOUNG MARY *(To GABRIEL)*   Go away.

MARY *(To GABRIEL)*   I'm newly married to Joseph. He's looking for me. His heart's breaking.

GABRIEL   Show the girl your wound.

MARY *(To YOUNG MARY)*   The rain's opening my wound like fruit. *(She opens her blouse. In between her breasts hangs a fruit like those in the trees. She opens the fruit and inside is GABRIEL's three-eyed face. The small face speaks.)*

GABRIEL   The lord is with thee: blessed art thou among women. Fear not, for thou hast found favor with God.

YOUNG MARY *(To MARY)*   Run away.

MARY   Go home now. You've seen enough.

GABRIEL   And behold, thou shalt conceive in thy womb and bring forth a son, and shalt call his name Jesus. *(The head in the tree flies away. MARY hangs the fruit of her breasts in the tree.)*

MARY *(To* YOUNG MARY*)*   You can watch if you hide. Make a nest. Keep your eyes open.

GABRIEL *(From offstage)*   He shall be great, and shall be called Son of the Highest; and the Lord God shall give unto him the throne of his father David.

MARY *(To* YOUNG MARY*)*   Because I will marry God, I am greater than the angels. Because I translate God to the earth, I am greater than Christ. Because God desires me, I am greater than God.

YOUNG MARY   You haven't married him yet. *(*GABRIEL *enters, the boy working the puppet of himself from inside: a tiger's head with many eyes, and two mouths — a sword in his right hand and a slaughtered lamb in his left. Broad wings.)*

GABRIEL   And he shall reign over the house of Jacob forever; and of his kingdom there shall be no end.

MARY   How shall this be, since I know not a man?

GABRIEL   The Holy Ghost shall come upon thee, and the power of the Highest shall overshadow thee: therefore also that Holy thing which shall be born of thee shall be called the Son of God. For with God nothing shall be impossible.

MARY   Behold the handmaiden of the Lord. *(She sprouts golden wings and a ruby halo. Bright green birds flock about her and cheetahs appear under her feet. To God)* Be it unto me according to thy word. *(Music starts; she and the angel dance. She overpowers* GABRIEL*.)* My soul doth magnify the lord. And my spirit hath rejoiced in God my Savior. For he hath regarded the low estate of his handmaiden: for, behold, from henceforth all generations shall call me blessed. For he that is mighty hath done to me great things, and holy is his name. And his mercy is on them that fear him from generation to generation. He hath showed strength with his arm; he hath scattered the proud in the imagination of their hearts. He hath put down the mighty from their seats, and exalted them of low degree. He hath filled the hungry with good things, and the rich he has sent empty away. He hath holpen his servant Israel, in remembrance of his mercy: as he spoke to our fathers, and Abraham, and to his seed forever. *(The light goes on in the tower window.)*

ANNE   Come home. Finish your lesson. *(JOSEPH comes in, dressed in a carpenter's work clothes, carrying a tri-square in his right hand.)*

JOSEPH   Come home, Mary. You were teaching me how to read. *(GABRIEL exits, his job done. MARY devolves: attendants chase the birds and cheetahs away; the halo is removed. The wings are folded and bound with straps. A band is tied around MARY's forehead, and large crystal tears hang below her eyes.)* Don't cry. I love you. I'm your groom!

MARY *(To YOUNG MARY)*   Don't go home. You know too much now. When I go to the Ascension, it's your turn to come down and find a hiding place.

JOSEPH   Who are you talking to?

MARY   No one.

JOSEPH   Well. Come in soon. *(He exits. MARY takes a pose by the lake, and turns into a statue. The Annunciation — a stuffed dove is wired to her finger. YOUNG MARY, up in the tree, her face tightly framed by the branches, cups her hands and whistles like a mourning dove.)*

YOUNG MARY   Walking through the museum of myself, by the lake, careful not to shoulder the standing terra cotta and porcelain figures, I see very clearly: the background, flat and vivid in the water behind my suspended head. The tree, hands, birds, tears.

ANNE *(Far away)*   Mary? Mary?

YOUNG MARY   I stay in the tree, the involved roots cracking stone. The ripening tree, tightening. Lifting the nest, tightening, ripe. Baby tree, rocking me, enscripting its space. I am Mary. I am Mary.

RADIO ELEPHANT

(Barbara)

Characters

BARBARA

NARRATOR

PRIEST

FATHER

BOB

JO

DRYADS

SOLDIERS

This version of *Radio Elephant* was first performed at Sledgehammer Theatre in San Diego in June 1993, directed by Scot Feldsher. Producer: Ethan Feerst. Cast: Susan Gelman, Dana Hooley, Bruce McKenzie, Martin Namaro, Chava Burgueno, Lorena Santana, Julia D'Orazio, Newsha Farsi, Adam Latham, Christopher Montelongo, Todd O'Keefe. Production: Vince Mountain, Pierre Clavel, Christian Hertzog, Janis Benning, Katherine Ferwerda, Dave Cannon, Ethan Feerst, Beth Robertson, Adam Latham, Sara Walke, Christi Sibul, Al Germani, Scott Feldsher, Ricardo Canestrelli, Oreste Canestrelli, Chava Burgueno, Bruce McKenzie, Kathleen King, Amy Thornberry and Co., Denise Dorsey, Eric Ogilvie, Lisa Noelle Stone, Stacy Rae Roth, Victoria Petrovich, Chad Steven, Frank Baran, Guy Clemmons, Leigh Hastfield, Al Kane, George Karnoff, Bruce McKenzie, Erik Ogilvie, Peter Smith. Band: Guzoo (Michael Carpenter, Bruce McKenzie, Johnny Monroe).

All songs by Christian Hertzog/Erik Ehn. Original incidental music by Christian Hertzog, Tim Labor, Bruce McKenzie. Additional assistance by Pea Kicks, Erik Knutzen and Tim Labor.

BARBARA   Where I was. Eyes closed. A-1 head. My little chant: Hey-la-hey. Where I was alive. Silver signal passing into and out of me. The magnetic bee — me — in the middle of the buzz. My closed eyes seeing my open eyes. Head making head. All head and head. Head buried in the field. I am signal. Come in. *(Lights out on her, and she exits. Downstage left, a girl at a desk. She's in a Catholic schoolgirl's uniform; she's the* NARRATOR. *On the desk, a cup of tea, a radio, a notebook, and the* Big Picture Book of Saints. *Fiona Ritchie's "Thistle and Shamrock" show plays on the radio.)*

NARRATOR   A desk, a cup of tea, a notebook, a radio and the *Big Picture Book of Saints.* I say what I see, and what you see, because I am open, honest, and intelligent. Saint Barbara. *(She opens the book.* BARBARA *is in the tower with a* JESUIT. BARBARA's *father makes his way to the tower.)* I have read these things. And everything I know through reading is true.

BARBARA *(To* JESUIT*)*   Where does it go? If it turns around, where's the axis?

JESUIT   I'm as tight as a tick.

BARBARA   Start over if you have to. Where do you want to go with this?

JESUIT   The headaches are very bad.

BARBARA   Face me.

JESUIT   The headaches are very bad. I don't know why you ask me these questions.

BARBARA   I don't mean any disrespect.

JESUIT   I can't go on and on. Your father — *(*FATHER *knocks)*

FATHER   Barbara?

NARRATOR   Barbara's father locked her in a tower when she turned thirteen. Many handsome princes wanted to marry her, and her father didn't want to let her go. But Barbara wanted to become a saint. So she smuggled in religious sages. How? *(Looks up)* How did they get in there? How did she ever get what she needed? *(She makes corrections.)* Barbara was very beautiful, and was locked in a tower. She saved all her dinner napkins and made a rope ladder for a man who taught her how to smuggle information when caught up in captivity. *(The* JESUIT *exits. The* FATHER *stays. A ladder leans. A drum roll. A Native American in a cut-off flannel shirt, jeans, boots, and a baseball cap climbs up.)*

BOB   I'll teach you how to build a radio.

FATHER *(To* BARBARA*)*   I have to talk to you.

NARRATOR   She did not need the company of men. She did not need the company of men or women.

BOB   I've contacted them. They have your coordinates. You're missing a crystal. I'll bring it next time.

BARBARA   Mr. Arrington?

BOB   Call me Bob.

BARBARA   How does it work? How does it all come together?

FATHER *(Knocking)*   Barbara?

NARRATOR   Sh. *(Correcting)* She needed—Barbara was locked in a tower by her father when she had her first period. Her father believed that if she was grounded, if she was on the ground and her blood was allowed to enter the earth, that she would conduct electricity, that she would attract powerful forces. So her father suspended her between heaven and earth. But she required neither heaven nor the earth. Barbara learned genius from secret women. From Jo Arrington, the wife of the Indian who built the world's first radio in Barbara's tower. Barbara's hair grew at a fantastic rate during her time of the month, and this is how Jo climbed up.

JO   The missing gem is an egg of turquoise. Veins of a color you've never identified. Very smooth. The voices of the ancestors and their babies come in, come in.

BARBARA   I can almost see the radio waves, Jo. Like dragonfly wings. I can feel them working in this room. Working in me like infection, like exception to the rule. And I'm a monster full of radio. I touch my tongue to the toaster and I hear an illegal Korean station singing and announcing in a language I don't know, but all that I don't know is becoming easier and easier to understand, even though I still don't know it, because I am transforming. My head. Job's disease — elephantiasis. The elephant head radio girl. Infinite ears. Intuition.

JO   Your intuition can't be that good. you can't know what I know as well as you pretend.

BARBARA   Shut the window. Bar the door from the inside. You'll be the beautiful lady and I'll be the wonder in the circus to come. *(The tower closes.)*

NARRATOR   She was afraid of her head. Afraid of her head changing shape, and the big ears.

FATHER   I know you're in there. It's not good. What you're doing, learning to read, and reading what you're reading . . . it's not good. They've put a warrant out for your arrest, dear. If it comes to trial they'll have your head. Explain it.

NARRATOR   Or —

FATHER   You're under arrest. I've come to behead you, dear. You don't listen. *(The tower opens.* JO *and* BARBARA *are dressed in sequins — circus clothes.)*

BARBARA   I can escape by high wire, dad. Radio equals head-circus. I know my way around.

NARRATOR   Or— *(The tower closes.)*

FATHER   What am I gonna do with you? *(He gets down on his knees.)* I don't pray like you do, but I pray, I pray. What am I gonna do with you, kid? I know what I am going to do with you. I'm old enough to have done this plenty of times, and seem to recall now that ancient justice always concludes one step beyond the satisfaction of any one person's cause. You come up against me with these things you've learned. You die. But this is not the conclusion. The one step further: I die for killing you. *(Rising)* Come out and play, Barbara. Elephant girl, come out. *(The tower opens. BARBARA's hair is brilliant about her. She has the ears of an elephant.)*

NARRATOR   She never escapes the tower but is allowed to leave with Bob when he proposes. She leaves after her first period and lives as a celibate. She never leaves the tower and wastes away to nothing. She escapes and is tracked down.

BARBARA *(To her FATHER)*   I can run away in a style that makes you chase me. *(JO goes down to the ground, and BARBARA goes out of the tower onto a tightrope. JO is the beautiful lady: she displays events, rides horseback, bends over backwards to pick up a shot glass with her tongue, etc.)*

NARRATOR   She runs in terror from the sword her father tries to hide. She runs in terror from the sword the guard displays. She walks without hesitation into a stone room with gutters and buckets. She runs smiling into the woods, the circus of signals swelling the figure's head.

BARBARA   I hide my blood in the mountains. I will repose my soul in the trees. *(Dryads)*

JO   Dryads! You're in luck. *(BARBARA is made a Dryad; the NARRATOR joins the assembly.)*

BARBARA and the DRYADS
Memorize a vowel
Head blown out
Hair the great eastern wind
Teeth bite waves
   I hide my blood in the mountains
   I repose my soul in the trees
Read by rote
Route revealed
Resistance arch, humpback heaven
Radio rainbow, muscles of Atlas
   I hide my blood in the mountains
   I repose my soul in the trees
Job's bones blistering —
Elephantiasis. Tightrope
   I hide my soul in the mountains
   I repose my soul in the trees

BARBARA   Sometimes my body hides in the trees and my soul runs
ahead to find a safe place. Sometimes my father is chasing only my body.

BARBARA/NARRATOR   He is confused in the circus of possibilities. The
head on my body is of such monstrousness now that he doesn't know
how to approach it.

BOB   I have a way to make you safe.

JO   She's over here now, Bob. See how well she's doing?

BOB   Okay. *(He begins a chant under his breath.)*
Redeemer Receiver
In hoc signal
Every hour
Is Magneto Paraclete, O —
Ra pro nobis
Come in tower

Dot dot dot dot dot dot dot
Dash dash dash dash dash
If this were an actual emergency
Lightning's cash would flash

NARRATOR   Our visions have stolen our tongues and are working them now, making such a racket that pops and the patrol find us. Our body is hidden away under the mountain, and our soul goes up to the tree branches to watch. *(To the* FATHER*)* Now's the time. It's hard to wait. *(He hesitates.)* Three separate openings into eternity. Use them in a story so that one leads to another. Your sword, our blood, the lightning. Line them up, and you'll have your path through to the end.

FATHER   I find her hiding in the brambles. I cut her loose with my sword to carry her away from the death squad. But she pricks her thumb on a thorn. When her blood enters the earth, lightning strikes me dead.

NARRATOR *(Correcting him)*   Your sword, our blood. *(*BARBARA *falls from the tree. She's unsteady.)*

DRYADS   Barbara's mind becomes light as a balloon, for a time line long as a balloon string, watching the coming of the severing of her head.

BARBARA *(To* NARRATOR*)*   Jo, what does this word mean?

NARRATOR   I'm not Jo, Barbara.

FATHER   I hear the guards drag you out and I turn the sword on myself.

NARRATOR   Your sword and *our* blood. One flows from the other.

FATHER   And then she kills herself with the same sword.

NARRATOR   As soon as she picks it up it's *her* sword.

BARBARA   Jo, what does this word mean?

JO   It means you never get away.

BARBARA *(To BOB)*   When will I die?

BOB   Very soon.

BARBARA/NARRATOR   It's hard to wait.

FATHER   I kill her in the cradle before her beautiful, beautiful head deforms.

BARBARA *(Balance returns; she's back to her place in the story.)*   But I am big in the head. I have plenty of room to die in. You chose your windows a long time ago. Put them in a row.

DRYADS   Lastly:

FATHER   I took my daughter to a cave, when she made her protest against the menstrual laws that confine women to huts poled up so they will ride between heaven and earth through the first year of the cycle. I knew she would be killed for this, and I didn't want her to die at the hands of a stranger.

BARBARA *(To NARRATOR)*   He hears the royal guard. The Dryads hold them back as along as possible. *(Burly guards jog heavily through the woods.)*

DRYAD   He swings and the head flies off. The blood enters the earth. The earth drains it quickly.

NARRATOR   Nothing happens. The silence makes the man queasy. He drives the sword into the wall of the cave, wiping it clean, killing time — and the blood off the sword is the word to God's wrath. Lightning cracks the mountain down and buries the father alive. It's not the blood of the girl, but the blood of the girl's murder that conducts electricity. And girls are murdered all the time. *(The FATHER stands for a moment, on fire.)*

BARBARA *(To the NARRATOR, as all others leave)*   My father kills me in the woods, and I see myself leaving my story. My soul reposes in the branches, and I am as a fly to my own butchered parts. I seize the hope that all my soul can fit in my turning, separate head, and I throw myself out. I am entirely in my skull, and we float, electric-eyed, smiling, turning. My hair doesn't drag on the ground anymore, and the number of waves sent and received is infinite. Time and space are impossible in the field of me. *(A representation of* BARBARA*'s handsome, monstrous head rises and revolves, self-illuminated, in bliss. The rest of* BARBARA *leaves. the* NARRATOR *composes herself and returns to her desk. "Thistle and Shamrock" again.)*

NARRATOR   I read the story of Saint Barbara on a school night, listening to Fiona Richie on the radio. Everything I hear on the radio late at night is everything I read and understand; is all true. In an apartment on the Grand Concourse, the Bronx, the present, I reach for my high Barbara.

THE FREAK
(George)

Characters

GUNNA

KNIGHT

The Freak was first performed at BACA in Brooklyn as part of the series' premiere, March 1990, directed by Fritz Ertl. Artistic Directors: Bonnie Metzher, Thalia Field. Other Series Directors: Thalia Field, Jennifer McDowall, Brian Mertes, Bonnie Metzger, and Randolyn Zinn. Cast: Maja Hellmold, Phoebe Kreutz, David Alton. Production: Pat Chanteloube, Barbara Cohig, Betsy Finston, John Gromada, Lora Pennington, Peter Hine, Charlotte Kreutz, David Woolard, Karen Dillon, Amanda Junquera, Kyle Chepulis, Stephen Kellam, Dawn Groenewegen.

Scene One: Girl with Wings

(A woman in a Swedish teacher's uniform sits on a stool downstage right. The only light on stage is a large spot on the upstage wall; in the circle: the shadow of a moth, flying furiously.)

NARRATOR   In 1957 in Stockholm, Sweden, a girl was born with wings. She was quick and mortal as a bee; her wings moved at a bee's rate. The doctor didn't know what to say, although he tried to piece together several different set speeches on death and deformity and the wonder of life, and the nonaccountability of the hospital. The mother, on the other hand, was quite happy with her new daughter, whom she named Gunna. Gunna flew in one spot in the center of the room, as if a ball of light were there, and flew and flew until her smiling mother opened her arms, held and nursed her, the silky membranes of her still moist wings flexing gently now, in time to her life-loving breathing. *(Light fades.)*

Scene Two: Classroom

(Lights up. An austere classroom; the sound of young men and women shouting. A teacher's voice over them: "Class! Class!" In midair, the puppet of the ten-year-old GUNNA flies with large white wings.)

NARRATOR   Gunna was very popular with her classmates. Her parents sewed special vents in her uniform that allowed for the free exercise of her now great wings. She would not be daunted. In the middle of a recitation, she would take to the air. The other boys and girls would try to touch her, or even a piece of her clothing when she was in these ecstasies, hoping that they would wake up the next day with the same abilities. Even the teacher found her hand lifting slightly to the shoes of the girl making the turn in front of her. At the same time, Gunna was not neglectful of her studies. On the contrary. Life held so many possibilities for her that she wanted to know all about it: about its past, present, and future, about teeth and sins and towns. She would stay up all hours drinking espresso coffee and shifting hats on her head, talking rapidly with her parents on the highest plane. *(Lights fade.)*

Scene Three: The Dream

(Lights up on a real GUNNA *in bed late at night.)*

NARRATOR: One night Gunna had a dream. *(*GUNNA *gets out of bed and flies slowly downstage. Lights up on a room in a medieval castle, with straw on the floor. A young man in chain mail sits in the corner. He looks up sadly.)*

KNIGHT   You're too late.

GUNNA   For what?

KNIGHT   I died a long time ago.

GUNNA   What do you want?

KNIGHT   I want to be a saint.

GUNNA   Do you deserve to be?

KNIGHT   I've been very virtuous. It would mean so much to me.

GUNNA   What's keeping you?

KNIGHT   A few things. Mostly though, I haven't been baptized.

GUNNA   Why not?

KNIGHT   A horrible oversight.

GUNNA   I can help you.

KNIGHT   Too late?

GUNNA   I can baptize you right now.

KNIGHT   Can you?

GUNNA   Oh—but I can't touch you, if you're in another time.

KNIGHT   Could you baptize a part of me?

GUNNA   Give me your shoe. Try passing it over to me.

NARRATOR   The knight took off his metal shoe, and, with serious effort, pushed it across the floor of the cell. *(A loud pop)* The article made it through the invisible pane of time and appeared in Gunna's present.

KNIGHT   You can't perform the sacraments yourself, can you?

GUNNA   Won't it be good enough? I have a jackknife.

KNIGHT   It has to be official.

GUNNA   I'll see what I can do.

KNIGHT   You'll come back?

GUNNA   Of course. *(She crosses back to bed.)*

NARRATOR   When she woke up, she had a shoe. *(Lights fade.)*

Scene Four: Pope of Rome

(Lights up on GUNNA *in flight. Her wings are decorated with gold. She flies earnestly.)*

NARRATOR   She told no one, but went straight to the Pope of Rome, looking her best. Her fame was such that she was granted an immediate audience. An archbishop at the pope's left ear expressed serious misgivings. But the pontiff smiled continuously at Gunna, assuring her that baptism by proxy was quite the norm. He sprinkled the shoe with some of Gunna's very own blood, drawn from her thumb with her jackknife. Translated by the pope, this was all made to seem on the up and up. Gunna flew off, but with no smile. She flew very thoroughly, so that she would sleep deeply enough to reach the knight again and rise to any new challenge, strong in her dream. She could not hear the archbishop almost raise his voice. She could not hear the pope quiet his ally by saying:

VOICE OF THE POPE   They look on her as on an angel. But she is just a girl with wings. The freak! *(Lights out.)*

Scene Five: Back to the Dream

(Lights up on the girl in bed. She rises.)

NARRATOR   She— *(GUNNA holds a finger to her lips and quiets the NARRATOR. GUNNA crosses to the cell. The KNIGHT is ill and holds his bare foot.)*

GUNNA   Tell me what happened.

KNIGHT   Give me my shoe.

GUNNA   You've hurt yourself. Tell me how. I'm taking care of you.

KNIGHT   Then give me my shoe. *(She passes it to him with effort. The KNIGHT struggles to put it on.)*

GUNNA   Your foot's swollen. Wearing the shoe gives you a horrible expression. You look like an old man.

KNIGHT   There is a civil war outside. I was called to combat while you were out. *(GUNNA finds an arrow in the straw.)*

GUNNA   This arrow—

KNIGHT   It's poisoned. They shot me in the heel. I wasn't running away. They were all around us. I'm dying now.

GUNNA   It's all been arranged, about the baptism. You're all right. They'll make you a saint when you die.

KNIGHT   There's something else I need.

GUNNA   Consider it done. Sit down. You're working the poison through.

KNIGHT   I've had an unremarkable life. With no conquests. Do you know where you are now?

GUNNA   I'm in the dream.

KNIGHT   Since your blood is on the shoe, you're on my side of the time pane for as long as the dream lasts.

GUNNA   I'll appear behind you in a battle — they'll take me as a sign.

KNIGHT   The honor of the moment would be conferred on you, unless I carried the day. And I'm not feeling very well. Speaking plainly, I am not an especially good knight.

GUNNA   There must be some advantage to my being here.

KNIGHT   I need to accomplish a miracle. I doubt in my ability to make something good. Perhaps I can destroy something evil.

GUNNA   Like a dragon.

KNIGHT   That works. I'll show them the dragon's wings.

GUNNA   I'm awake. I'm awake now.

KNIGHT   No, you're not. You're deep, deep asleep. (GUNNA *flies, thumping around the cell.*)

GUNNA   These wings are beautiful. They won't believe they're from a dragon.

KNIGHT   They'll be covered in blood. Terrible. The wings are mine when I take them. You're too strange to live.

GUNNA   What's your name?

KNIGHT   George.

GUNNA   You're Saint George, then. Yes, the dragon slayer. It all comes true. *(The* KNIGHT *pulls* GUNNA *down and cuts off her wings.* GUNNA *returns to bed.)*

NARRATOR   When she woke up, her wings were gone. *(Lights fade.)*

Scene Six: The Narrator

(Lights up on a classroom.)

NARRATOR   I have never flown since, even in my dreams. But I do remember. I teach in the room where I once flew, helping students with their penmanship. Damn saint stole my wings! But I walk the aisles, looking for young ones whose shoulders are especially hunched. For many of our girls and boys are born with wings, more than you know. But the parents follow a strict and loving instinct — they tie the wings back with strips of sturdy leather. When my wings were lopped, I was suddenly able to remember a thousand conversations that took place on the edge of my hearing — I didn't know I had heard these things until they all rushed at me at once. Pious speculations, and outright hate. The pope's word, "Freak," finally made its way to my ears. When I find a hunched student, a good one, I call this creature in for extra work, and I take out my jackknife, and cut slits for the wings. The problem is not the wings, I say. The problem is not the wings. *(The shadow of a baby with wings flies upstage in a circle of light.)*

CEDAR

(John of the Cross)

Characters

JOHN OF THE CROSS

MAN

BIRD

GIRL GUADALUPE

WOMAN GUADALUPE

WOMAN

Cedar is unproduced.

Scene One: Stand Up!

(Two men squat.)

OFFSTAGE VOICE *(male)*   Stand up! *(The men do. One* MAN *finds himself in a cardboard, scale model town. The sun — a yellow-gelled flashlight on a clothesline — follows him wherever he goes. The town surrounds the ten by six prison cell of the other man —* JOHN OF THE CROSS. *Moonlight shines down on* JOHN's *head; the moon's a clear light bulb frozen in a block of ice and hung from the neck of a star by a wire.* JOHN *is bound and can't rise completely.)*

MARY'S VOICE   The sun off his fontanel and the moon off his fontanel, at two in the afternoon, two at night. Driving towards two, all day, all night. *(The men reach their hands up to their light sources. Blackout.)*

Scene Two: While My Freedom Walks through Town

(Early evening in the cell, early morning in the city. JOHN *is stretched out on his floor; the* MAN *stands as he did. A* BIRD *whose feathers show the colors of the* VIRGIN OF GUADELOUPE *comes to the bars of the prison window.)*

BIRD, JOHN   While my freedom walks through town. *(The* MAN *moves; he takes careful, high-kneed steps through the model.)*

JOHN   I see him reflected in your pupil, bird. *(Blackout)*

Scene Three: That One May Come on Randomly

(The cell is dark; prostrate JOHN *trembles. The* MAN *kills time; his hands are empty. He repeats part of his journey; he tries to judge time by the sun, which is behind a cloud; he picks a house, kneels, and looks through a tiny window. A* WOMAN *upstage acts out what he sees: she pours milk on cereal; she puts her hair behind her ear.)*

MAN   Did I ever live here? *(Her back is to him; she doesn't move once her hand touches her ear. The milk overflows the bowl.)*

BIRD *(Lingering)*   The accident and foreknowledge of the accident are in love with one another. *(The* WOMAN *cries. The* BIRD *exits.)*

MAN   Don't cry. Is it so sad? *(A ten-year-old* VIRGIN OF GUADELOUPE *comes on. She has a paper bird on a string, suspended from a long stick; she whirls it over the* MAN's *head. He only sees the bird, not* GUADELOUPE. *Sharp noises: cut air.)* Wires are gathered by a gear in my chest — they are twisted to a cello string — the string God uses to hang birds from the sky. Jay, go home! *(*JOHN *springs up as best he can, and bashes against the walls of the cell.)*

Scene Four: Circular Discipline

*(*GIRL GUADELOUPE *finishes and goes home. The* WOMAN *appears at a church kneeler. The* MAN *lowers a kneeler of his own — "squeak." The* MAN *prays.)*

MAN   Don't leave. Don't leave. Don't leave. *(She doesn't. A wheel on which restaurant orders are pinned circles over* JOHN. JOHN, *in a crouch, no power in his hands, pulls an order off with his mouth, and drops it to the floor. He reads.)*

WOMAN   Beat till fluffy. Dry grill. They beat him so severely his shoulders will never be the same. Streams of blood down his back: cut puppet strings. *(The* MAN *thinks maybe she is talking to him, but* GIRL GUADELOUPE *enters dressed in contemporary clothes and kneels next to the* WOMAN; *the* GIRL *is the conversational partner.* JOHN *writes in blood on the back of the check;* GIRL GUADELOUPE *leans forward and reads what* JOHN *writes.)*

GIRL GUADELOUPE   "Circular discipline. The friars, my jailers, walk a circle around me in the heresy cell; each man strikes me with a leather scourge." *(Blackout)*

Scene Five: Church

(The MAN *remains kneeling. He looks up and observes that the* WOMAN *is gone; the* GIRL *spies upstage but the* MAN *doesn't see her.* JOHN *lies still. A cello note. The* MAN, *still kneeling, moves as if metal fibers where being pulled through his chest and twisted to a cello string. He breathes. Blackout)*

Scene Six: Virgin of Guadeloupe Torn Through

(The WOMAN *appears to* JOHN *as the Virgin of Guadeloupe. Her live face appears through a hole in a painting of her icon. She falls through. Her robe is ragged. Her back is bare, and welted. She's bound.* JOHN *and* WOMAN GUADALUPE *come to one another, squat-standing, bird-like. They take turns biting each other's knots. The* MAN *prays in church.)*

MAN   Honey so pure it flows from the spoon slick as clear alcohol.
(Mary and JOHN *slow down, but don't stop.)*

Scene Seven: Feeling Mary's Eyes

*(*WOMAN GUADELOUPE *stands.* JOHN *still stands in a squat, even though his ropes are gone.* GIRL, *as a holy thing, tends to the* WOMAN. *She stitches cuts leading back from the grown-up's eyes along either side of the head. The* GIRL *bites the thread, and leaves.)*

JOHN   She walks through walls?

WOMAN GUADALUPE   She's my angel.

JOHN *(Re: the cuts)*   How — ?

WOMAN GUADALUPE   They cut me in strange places. They tried to cut my eyes. But since they were only men, everything they did was in the past, and their movements were sluggish. I turned my head as gentle as this— *(She shows)* And the knife they shared between them glanced off this side, then this side. Feel them. *(JOHN does. Blackout)*

Scene Eight: Missing Church

(The MAN is less upright at the kneeler. He's bored, but wants to stay in a church state of mind. He flips through the missal, practices the Nicene Creed, tries to see if he can remember the Latin for the Agnus Dei, runs down a hymn. Phantom kneeler-squeak. He turns whenever he hears it, but discovers nothing. Then, from out of a hillside graveyard in the scale model city pops the GIRL as girl. Her two hands are folded into one fist in front of her. She prays.)

GIRL   Here is the church, here is the steeple. Open the door, and here are God's people. *(She opens her hands and wriggles her interlaced fingers. Blackout)*

Scene Nine: I Am Dying of Love

(The MAN walks through town. WOMAN GUADALUPE and JOHN kneel where they knelt when JOHN felt WOMAN GUADALUPE's eyes. They hold hands.)

JOHN   You've come to help me escape.

WOMAN GUADALUPE   This is Ubeda, not Toledo. We tied bed sheets in Toledo for you to climb down!

JOHN   Can't you help me?

WOMAN GUADALUPE   I can, but not to escape. Ubeda is a harder place. See— my icon is in tatters.

JOHN   Then what have you come to help me do?

WOMAN GUADALUPE   To die in here, John. John of the Cross. *(They embrace. The* GIRL *enters. The* MAN *doesn't see her.)*
Muerome de amores
carillo, que hare?

GIRL   Que te mueras, alahe!

WOMAN GUADALUPE   Cede.

Scene Ten: Old

(Sun and moon shine on the MAN *and* JOHN.*)*

JOHN   But my freedom walks —

WOMAN GUADALUPE   You are here and you are there, in the room, out of the room. Here, you are dying. Just because you are dying doesn't mean you don't still walk through the city. *(The* MAN *follows the* GIRL *around trying to tell her a story.* JOHN *and* WOMAN GUADALUPE *wash each other's feet.)*

MAN   I kill time waiting for daily mass to start down at St. Joseph the Worker. I walk; don't know the neighborhood; look in the kitchen windows. I can smell the milk with my imagination. It isn't my milk; it isn't my mess . . . why cry? I circle back to the church. Still early. A good building — plain windows; nice dimensions and a well-lit shrine to the Holy Family. A woman's there. She prays the rosary next to her daughter. I scare her off when I squeak the kneeler. I wait, I wait, and no mass. Passing a double door to a chapel on the way out, frosted glass, I smell chapel candles. I swear the place wasn't there when I came in. *That's* where they have the daily service, no bigger than a six by ten. I've missed it. Go to the Post Office to see about a check. Not there. Go to the library, tilt the silver urn over a Styrofoam cup.

GIRL   Dose.

MAN   Up into the stacks. Try to find a book on Racer X — Speed Racer's brother.

GIRL   He was always my favorite.

MAN, GIRL   Come on a book of poems by John of the Cross.

MAN   Poems about hearing at night — seeing better at night. Eat a bag lunch in a plaza where they have a compass embedded in the concrete. I am delaying to put flyers up. I'm waiting for Racer X. I think Racer X is Joseph the Worker. I think the way Christ is not a bastard is that Joseph and Mary are both God, and that Joseph slept with his Mary half in a way that did her no damage and then forgetfulness. Old. John of the Cross is going to put an "x" on Joseph's head so I'll know he's Racer X and I can stop speed racing. *(Blackout)*

GIRL   Up.

Scene Eleven: Cedar

(JOHN puts an "x" on the GIRL's forehead; she is dressed as Joseph the Worker. The MAN has lost track of her; he looks for her, but she's always just behind him. The MAN takes off his shoes and walks out of the bounds of the city. Tree shadows slip.)

GIRL   A stand of cedars in a park downtown.

MAN   Can't keep the coffee down. Oh, I am a flower, yes.

WOMAN GUADALUPE   Two in the afternoon, two at night. Moon and sun on fontanel.

MAN   Cedars sharper than flowers. Shadow writes on sun's white.

WOMAN GUADALUPE   Cedar light in the cell.

GIRL   On the way to post flyers.

WOMAN GUADALUPE   Our babies collapsing.

JOHN   Brush pulses —

MAN   And I am —

JOHN   Suspended in dark

MAN   In light

WOMAN GUADALUPE   In hair

GIRL   In air. *(Parallels: The* MAN *turns and stands before the* GIRL, JOHN *before* WOMAN GUADALUPE. JOSEPH *and* WOMAN GUADALUPE *brush the pulses of their loved ones.* JOHN *and the* MAN *close their eyes.)*

Scene Twelve: Sweet Smell

*(*JOHN *lies dead in his cell. The* MAN *lies dead in the park.* WOMAN GUADELOUPE *kneels by* JOHN; *the* GIRL, *as Joseph the Worker, kneels by the* MAN.*)*

WOMAN/GIRL   He smells sweet. *(*WOMAN *and* GIRL *dismember the corpses.)*

WOMAN GUADALUPE   Feet to Barcelona. Fingers to Avila. Shins to Toledo. Arms to Grenoble. Head in Ubeda. The trunk, lost. Cedar lined trunk preserves heart. *(Flyers start to blow.)*

GIRL   Flyers spread, seeding. Wind. Where the trees stop, lilies grow — their spade-shaped leaves dark green. Flyers gather there.

WOMAN, GIRL   He with lilies sleeps.

CONTEMPLACION

(Mary and Martha)

Characters

Contemplacion is unproduced. It was written for the Playwrights Project, Dallas, Texas (Raphael Parry, Artistic Director).

Prologue

(A dark stage. A malnourished BOY *squats in a small chicken-wire cage that hangs midway between floor and ceiling. The cage is lightly electrified; the* BOY *swipes a wire bristle brush across the mesh, and the sparks make the only light.)*

BOY   Make the bed. Kill the boy. Hang the maid. Flower of Contemplation. *(Quiet and dark again)*

Scene One: Make the Bed

(The cage is gone; fluorescent light. The broad black floor is under six inches of water. FLOR CONTEMPLACION, *the mortal maid, walks through the water and unfolds a white sheet. A shaft of natural sunlight drops: a diagonal architecture. The same light transects the sheets and floors of heaven, where* MARY *and* MARTHA *make the angels' beds.* FLOR *prays to the sunlight.)*

FLOR   In your angle of light, oh my soul, I make the bed, amen. *(*VOICES *break through.)*

VOICE ONE   Flor, come in here.

FLOR   Float the sheet, ankle deep, good morning.

VOICE TWO   She hears you.

VOICE ONE   Flor?

FLOR   Hydroponic maid, hothouse rootless; oh flower opens in your hands, oh I find anchor in your touch.

VOICE TWO   She hears you.

FLOR *(Still to the light)*   How natural light cuts through the fluorescence. How the white is made material by your honesty. And the settling of the sheet is the plan of inscape.

VOICE ONE   Help me, Flor. I've lost everything.

FLOR   Love, love, your light's angle isolates my head in shadow on the white sheet—solitary ideogram. *(She spreads the sheet over the water tension. To* VOICE ONE*)* You will sleep on this. My graphic shadow defines your material world. *(The* BOY *appears in his cage; the cage approaches the water; stops just above the maid. The* BOY *sings.)*

BOY
    Flor Contemplacion is hung in Singapore
    Flor you will not sleep anymore
    Feet, hoist, can't find the floor
    Isolat face, the Maid of Singapore

FLOR   Soul in sun, see the bed they make me make. Mister, read my head, marked on morning's textile. *(Blackout)*

Scene Two: Kill the Boy

(The cage is gone. The BOY *stands in the water to one side of the sheet; he takes off his clothes, folds them, and sets them in the water.* FLOR *kneels in the water on the other side of the sheet. The* BOY *steps onto the sheet as if into a tub. He's taking a bath.* FLOR *cleans him. On a small sand atoll,* MARTHA *testifies into a microphone.)*

MARTHA   He was not in the house at the time—

FLOR, MARTHA   The father—

MARTHA   Came in and found him murdered.

FLOR   Comes in and finds you in the tub. You will be dead in a moment, sweet boy. Don't be afraid. I want you smiling when I join you. In Singapore today—

MARTHA   The maid, Flor Contemplacion —

FLOR   Is hanged for the murder of a rich man's son and housekeeper.

MARTHA   He was not in the house at the time. The father —

FLOR   Is a stranger to his promise. His four-year-old son — that's you — has an epileptic seizure in the bathtub. *(The* BOY *begins to wrap himself in the sheet, head to toe.)*

BOY   Wire scrub chicken wire nerves. Smother white sheet plain day. Flor?

FLOR   I am not here either, remember? If I were with you in the world, I would save you. I haven't seen my four children back in the Philippines in four years. The four years in you is the water of all my precious babies. I would not break the vessel, child. I would save you at the cost of my own life. They will not have to wash your skin to bury you. Your skin glows with spices, by magic.

BOY   My strength lapses on water.

FLOR   Boy, you are expiring light. Light bounces off these surfaces and travels away. *(Light fades.)*

Scene Three: Hang the Maid

(The BOY *sits cross-legged in the middle of the water, the sheet tight around him. A carnation unfolds in his upturned palms.* FLOR *hangs in the air above him; not by the neck, but by ropes to her shoulders.* MARTHA *is still on her island.* VOICE ONE *— Dad — kneels next to the* BOY *where* FLOR *just prayed. He replays both sides of a conversation he remembers.)*

DAD   Flor, come in here./She hears you.

ALL BUT DAD   Not as it was. *(MARTHA steps away from the microphone and crawls through the water.)*

FLOR   These words were put in her mouth. She chokes on water/ words. *(*MARY *enters and takes* MARTHA's *place at the mic.)*

DAD *(Up to* FLOR*)*   Flor, you've killed my son. Flor, you killed my housekeeper too.

BOY   Saying that a maid for a maid. He causes them to make his bed, he will cause them to lie in it.

DAD   Martha refused to carry a package of yours back to the Philippines on her last trip home. So you killed her and my son. *(*MARTHA *floats dead in the water.)*

BOY   He found me dead in the tub. Martha was not in the house at the time, but he waited for her and took her life to cash out pain's account.

FLOR   He missed the moment of the boy's dread need and put Martha's dead body in the place of his error. He then stood —

BOY   Stood in red water and watched them hang Flor Contemplacion for the murder of his maid and his son.

MARY   She was in my cell.

BOY   Many Filipinas work in Singapore. As with old Irish, chief export: workers' bodies.

MARY   Flor had been tortured.

BOY   Help often dies. Martha wore the clothes of the maid, Mary wears the clothes of —

FLOR   A prostitute in —

DAD *(Washing his hands)*   I confess —

BOY   Stood in red water. Could not clean. Stood and watched her hang.

FLOR   The prostitute in my cell —

BOY   Testifies:

VOICE TWO   She confesses under oath that the Flower's confession was tortured out. (DAD *searches the water.*)

DAD   It was right here.

FLOR   The father's torture will be confession itself. For he will have to confess one day, under heaven's circumstance.

DAD   Where did it go?

MARTHA   The woman paid to unmake beds testifies on behalf of the woman paid to make them. Flor Contemplacion was hanged in Singapore in March. She blooms solar carnation in the spring.

FLOR   The rope is from heaven because all things are from heaven.

BOY   Isolat face.

FLOR   Cut for grafting and rooted in heaven.

MARY   Turns to face —

FLOR   Turn to face the earth

MARTHA   Flower hangs in the sky. A flower grown for between God's beautiful breasts, for God's beautiful hair.

FLOR   The planet where the boy is buried.

BOY   Heaven's flower, stem thorough sky, rooted in sun, turns isolat face to follow the earth.

MARY   They are hung, flowers of death, flowers to make one think, eyes against the bandages and tongues bolting large.

FLOR   The rope can be from heaven. Grown hothouse on hearth, set firm in sky's wildness.

BOY   Heaven's flower lives on light.

BOY, FLOR   Satisfy my thirst with fire. *(Bright tongues)*

INCIDE

(Judas Iscariot)

Characters

SIMON

JUDAS

JUDAS' WIFE

WOMAN ONE

WOMAN TWO

MAN

Incide was first performed at the Annex Theatre in Seattle in April 1994, directed by the playwright. Artistic Director: Allison Narver. Cast: John Holyoke, Michael Shapiro, Heather Hughes, Allison Narver, Natache LaFerriere, Cynthia Whalen. Production: James Keene, Ken Judy, Jonathan P. Walker, Julie Vadnais, Carlos Trevino, Maximilian Bocek, Karl Gajdusek, Donald Crane, Tom Milewski, Andrew Lieberman, Heather Lewis, Suzanne Bybee, Gregory Musick, Margaret Doherty, Nancy Snapp, Kevin Mesher.

(A field of dry grass, early evening — a red/gold condition. Each blade of grass is free-standing — is a yard-long piece of wire stuck in a two-inch diameter concrete hemisphere; the blades wobble when a person walks through them. Stage left and stage right, church kneelers. Upstage, a huge crucifix hangs from chains. Two OLD WOMEN *kneel stage right. They say their rosaries and chat. An* OLD MAN *with clay-covered hands kneels left. Scene titles appear on a peg board on one side of the stage — the sort of board used to indicate hymn numbers in church.)*

Scene One: To the Stars

WOMAN ONE   The medicine is breaking her brain.

WOMAN TWO   On account of the cancer.

WOMAN ONE   She's losing weight.

WOMAN TWO   Isn't that a shame . . .

WOMAN ONE   Mary?

WOMAN TWO   Yes?

WOMAN ONE   Where do you put your prayers?

WOMAN TWO   To the stars. *(Small bells ring. Mass begins.* JUDAS ISCARIOT *crosses through the grass carrying a bowl of water. He kneels center and washes a hand. The others produce missals and read.)*

WOMEN and MAN   "He who has dipped his hand into the dish with me is the one who will betray me."

JUDAS *(Quoting from memory)*   "Surely it is not I, Rabbi."

WOMEN and MAN   "You have said so." *(*JUDAS *sprinkles water to the four points of the compass and then slops the rest around him. He rubs* *the tips of the index and middle fingers of his right hand inside the bowl to gather the last few drops. He crosses himself. Leans forward to kiss a phantom. The worshipers make a low reptilian hiss, the sound as formal and as memorized as the recited words. A policeman snakes his way through the grass.)*

MAN *(Whispering across to the* WOMEN*)*   Where do you send your prayers?

WOMEN   Sh. *(The* POLICEMAN *hands* JUDAS *a small sack.)*

POLICEMAN   Count it.

JUDAS   I can't count.

POLICEMAN   You can count to twelve, you can count to thirty.

JUDAS   I can minus one from twelve. I can minus thirty from thirty.

POLICEMAN   There's nowhere to put it. It can't be given over to the church treasuries — it's blood money.

WOMEN and MAN   "Each piece of silver shone — a matter-puncture letting light of God's hate through."

POLICEMAN   We killed him at twelve.

JUDAS   You don't know. It took him days to die.

POLICEMAN   We killed him at twelve, since that's a number he likes. At twelve years old. He's the moment. He's all his ages every second. We killed him as he was when he was a twelve-year-old boy. *(A twelve-year-old boy runs across, is shot, falls.)* Since a twelve-year-old boy is the most dead.

JUDAS   Take your money back.

POLICEMAN   There's no place it can go. It's not enough to worry about. It's the amount you compensate a slave owner when his property is gored by your ox.

MAN   You can't send your prayers to the stars since —

JUDAS *(Flinging the contents of the purse in a skyward arc; silver confetti)* I threw the I threw the — it's cold, dad. I threw the silver against the wall of the temple. The coins burned into the sky.

WOMEN and MAN   "The light of the coins stuck in heaven."

MAN   The piercings, the leaks of God's hate remained, and became the finest stars. The lusterless coins fell to the earth, stripped of their shine.

JUDAS   The priests gathered them.

MAN   Bought you a plot in potter's field, and buried you there.

JUDAS   Dad, it's cold. *(POLICEMAN and CHILD back off on their bellies, separately.)*

WOMEN, MAN   "Judas hung himself on a tree as Christ was hung from a tree."

MAN   But Judas was hung from the one point of his neck because Judas has only one point. He was dark matter between the stars that night. *(The MAN exits secretly.)*

JUDAS   You cannot pray to the stars because they are Judas silver. Our history, our small bagful, has been thrown out and has burned vents for God's hate. Our washing for eating, and our kissing, our two greatest intimacies with the world, have been bought too and thrown away. When we look to heaven we are praying to heavy Judas swinging across his silver.

WOMAN TWO   I saw that body too.

WOMEN ONE and TWO   The stars are Judas silver. And Potter's Field, the field of blood, shines between us. *(Blackout)*

Scene Two: To the Earth

(Evening, red/gold. The MAN *returns to his place, his hands still covered with clay. He's deep in prayer.)*

WOMAN ONE   He came back.

WOMAN TWO   His name is Simon.

WOMAN ONE   He's Simon Iscariot. Judas is his boy.

WOMAN TWO   He lost his wife. He's a widower.

WOMAN ONE *(Out to Audience)*   The title of this scene is "He Lost His Wife."

WOMAN TWO   No, it isn't. *(*WOMAN ONE *checks her missal and sees it isn't.)* Mary?

WOMAN ONE   Yes?

WOMAN TWO   Where do you send your prayers?

WOMAN ONE   Into the earth. *(Small bells ring. Mass begins.)*

WOMEN and SIMON   "Then all the disciples left and fled." *(*JUDAS *runs across, and is shot in the back. Dark of night.)*

SIMON *(In the dark)*   He was my son.

JUDAS and SIMON   I am looking for a quiet place. *(Dawn bumps up.)*

JUDAS   I want to be a farmer now.

LANDOWNER   You stink like fish.

JUDAS   I want a farm. My fingers aren't right for making the knots in the nets.

LANDOWNER   That's all right, I like fish. If I could retire I'd fish all day.

JUDAS   I got money. *(JUDAS pays the Landowner thirty pieces of silver and the LANDOWNER exits.)*

WOMEN and SIMON   "Lord God of all, you hand us over like sheep to be slaughtered, scatter us among the nations. Dear God you sell your people for nothing." *(JUDAS' wife enters, stands, and folds her arms, watching her husband.)*

SIMON *(Whispering)*   He wanted a safe place. He had a wife. He was my son. The new farmer scattered his seed like a child. His wife watched from the porch, arms folded, knowing only one man, knowing nothing would grow from their labor.

WOMAN TWO   Who do you have?

SIMON   My wife left. I am a potter. I open flaps of clay, and dream of hiding in gray envelopes of earth. Out of sight of the stars. My prayers go to the dirt.

WOMAN ONE   Judas opened the earth.

WOMAN TWO   And the earth would not take his seeds.

WOMAN ONE   Judas hated to repair the nets.

WIFE   Hated more to plow the clay.

SIMON   He fell across his plow and his insides opened out.

WOMEN and SIMON   "Falling headlong, he burst open in the middle and all his insides fell out."

SIMON   Old. *(JUDAS falls, plowing. His insides open out.)*

JUDAS   A safe place a safe place a plot with no trees for the high branch mockingbird no handle for baby's tantrum as you pull him away no boats for slipping and drowning no nets to tangle ground ground a safe place dull earth duller than sky's mirror, earth to take it, take it take it all I'm done, away, vented, out. Inside out.

WIFE   His wife remained, because here it is, knew the long and narrow stretch of day was shaped for a grave.

SIMON *(Crawling in symmetry with* JUDAS*)*   I crawl under a flap of clay.

WIFE   All my vessels break. I am a stranger to wine and grain.

JUDAS   Hold nothing. Safe place to be a sinner.

WOMAN ONE   The earth cannot take your prayers.

SIMON   The clay is a perfect grave. Hermetic.

WIFE   His body is intact.

SIMON   Clay cool and wet. Unfired.

WOMAN ONE   When you swim underground you swim with JUDAS.

JUDAS   For earth is the Judas purse.

WIFE   Its silver thrown against Heaven.

SIMON   Holds nothing but the cold and dead sinner.

WIFE   Mourner has no song, poem or quote, mind emptied for years by gazing on the fruitless plot. Says, in mourning: "Here it is."

WOMEN, SIMON   "The Earth is the Judas Purse."

WOMEN   And your prayers go to the planet's mummified fetish. *(Blackout)*

Scene Three: To Judas

(In the dark)

WOMEN, SIMON   Judas, speak.

WOMEN   "For creation was made subject to futility, not of its own accord —

SIMON   But because of the one who subjected it." *(Lights up.)*

WOMEN   With what do you sow your fields, Judas? *(JUDAS washes his hands in a bowl his WIFE holds.)*

JUDAS   I forbid myself daylight. Sow at night under the full moon. Old man. Loves smooth oats, but the smooth doesn't take the knives from the fisher's bones. I did not hang myself. The moon is hung, a Eucharist, and I labor under it's large exile. Nothing grows, sown at night. My wife can bear no children . . . But because of so many years at sea, I know how to be a sea horse, and carry my own children in my belly. For magic, I sow the earth with my children.

WIFE   When they say he opened in the middle, they mean he gave birth to a burst circle of children. He spewed them over his property.

JUDAS *(Spraying water out)*   And my children are salt in a gasoline placenta. The ground is poisoned. When I'm buried in it, daytime, my skin itches. I am buried in a corner of the field, under a turning-post for tractors, if tractors had reason to turn here. *(He lies down and dies. His WIFE strips his shirt off. She puts candles on his back, lights them, and extinguishes them by placing glass globes over them.)*

WIFE   I remember his coming in at night, the darkest-before-the-dawn time, as sore as could be. He sows at night under the Eucharist, which is hung amid the coins that purchased it. He comes in tired. There are thirty stars in heaven. I have counted them over and over. God has thirty eyes, all full of rage, each a knowledge of a piece of silver. Judas has arthritis and I trap heat over his sore muscles. But when he dies, he dies as clay in moonlight, old as he is cold. We have done too much and our children have done too much. We have killed our children and the graves of the children poison the soil. And it is all done under the sky, so the sky knows.

SIMON   All human prayers reach heaven through Saint Judas.

WOMEN   Saint Judas, pray for us.

WIFE   We have dried the earth to fetish, all prayer is to fetish.

WOMEN, SIMON   Saint Judas, pray for us.

WOMAN ONE   Saint Judas, I pray to you.

WOMEN, SIMON   Saint Judas, pray for us.

WIFE   We would kill our lover to fix a parking ticket.

WOMEN, SIMON   Saint Judas, pray for us.

WIFE   The earth is potter's field, is the Judas purse. And the stars are Judas silver. Eucharist hangs passive in its price. There is a field of blood between the kneelers. We pray on the floor of Akeldama.

ALL *(As the last candle on* JUDAS' *back is extinguished)*   Saint Judas, pray for us.

THE IMP OF SIMPLICITY

(Thomas à Kempis)

Characters

INGRID (future)

WILKIE (future)

SISTER ROBIN (the youngest)

SISTER MILAN (the oldest)

NUN 1 (slightly sees the future; identifies with WILKIE)

NUN 2 (ROBIN's secret friend)

NUN 3 (MILAN's secret friend)

NUN 4 (illiterate; fear and mouth)

NUN 5 (philosopher queen)

NUN 6 (loves PRINT)

NUN 7 (slightly sees the future; identifies with INGRID)

NUN 8 (quiet!)

NUN 9 (the Abbess)

NUN 10 (best with computers)

PRINT (present imperfect)

SINE QUA SI MODO

(without whom nothing much happens)

Choruses:

BELLS (pretty)

BIRDS (good insofar)

BATS (bad)

The Imp of Simplicity was first presented at Skidmore College, May 1997, directed by Scott Feldsher. It was written and developed through a residency sponsored by the Theatre Department, Gautam Dasgupta, Chair. Cast: Kelly Hamlin, Jessie Hawley, Gwyneth L. Dobson, Gabrielle Galanek, Laura Burns, Bernadette McHugh, Cate Owren, Erinn McCormack, Colleen Reily, Leah Buechley, Maggie Arndt, Allena Ruszkiewicz, Kathleen Cowan, Missy Compeau, Mark Doskow, Josh Chambers. Choruses: Cormac Bluestone, Julia Cerjanec, Amy Friedenberg, Tonia Georgakopoulou, Sue Kessler, Caroline Tye, Heather Connelly, Nicola Fordwood, Lydia Guiseffi, Prudence Heyert, Brian DePersia, Jeff Gilson, Richard M. Kern, Anne McFadden, Coleman O'Toole, Michael E. Smith.

Production: David Yergan, Garett E. Wilson, Jay Maury, Rachel Ehrlich, Maia Proujansky-Bell, Rebecca Smith, Ashley York Kennedy,

Ingrid Phillips, Zak Walshon, Amanda Dravecky, Matt Cosby, Daniel Ware, Matt Riva, Allison Becker, Patty Pawliczak, Edie Black, Julia Cerjanec, Hanna Duggan, Christopher Nakayama, Katie Platz, Nicole Raab, Alexis Ryan, Julia Zichello, Clayton Dowty, Sara Dodson, Michelle Gainski, Elizabeth Germo, Deanna Peace, Linda Tucker, Jon Bernthal, Cormack Bluestone, Patrick Brannan, Bill Caleo, Mike Comey, Heather Connelly, Mike Cornish, Gwyneth Dobson, Mark Doskow, Tim Fannon, Tonia Georgakopoulou, Kelly Hamlin, Billy Internicola, Andy Irons, Ben Kato, Bernadette McHugh, Jeff Menaker, Rebecca O'Neill, Brett Plymale, Alexis Ryan, Amy Schenck, Kate Spina, Kate Thomas, Jason Thomas, Daniel Ware, Aaron Williams, Marty Zentz, Jon Bernthal, Bill Caleo, Brian Cronin, Melissa Daroff, Chris Doherty, Justin Fayne, Michelle Person, Karin Rogers, Amy Schenk, Alex Siriani, Karina Valentine, Jennifer Cummings, Gillian Director.

Imitation of Christ references (even numbered scenes) are from Leo Shirley-Price's translation, Penguin Press, London, 1952. Bats and birds owed to Mac Wellman.

Scene One: Nitro Intro

NUN I   Sister Milan takes heart medicine.

MILAN   Robin. Wake up.

ROBIN   What?

NUN 2   Robin, wake up.

WILKIE   Sister Milan takes heart medicine.

NUN 3   Morning.

ROBIN   Morning.

NUNS 4, 5, 6, 7, 8, 9, 10 *(In sequence)*   Morning.

NUNS, INGRID, WILKIE   We are all waking up.

WILKIE   You see?

ROBIN   What?

MILAN   Sister Robin.

NUN 6   She's calling for you.

WILKIE   The oldest for the youngest.

INGRID   Like lamps.

NUN 7   She likes to take her nitro glycerin on an empty stomach.

NUN 8   Wakeful face by a broken backed book —

INGRID   Book down butchered by a light-filled glass of water.

MILAN   Sister Robin.

WILKIE   A secret.

ROBIN   In the future —

WILKIE   What?

ROBIN   What?

INGRID, WILKIE   Birds.

NUN 9   What?

ROBIN   In the future science fiction will want to come back and know all about us.

NUN 10   Why?

MILAN   Because we'll be gone.

INGRID   So old.

WILKIE   And gone.

MILAN   The birds in the trees will be made out of gold.

ROBIN   What?

MILAN   Made out of gold.

NUNS   And their songs will be adjectives over gold.

ROBIN   Beer will grow on trees.

NUN 1   And stars will come straight out of your head.

NUNS 3, 7, 9   And they will dream about us.

NUNS 2, 5, 6, 10   When we're gone.

PRINT   Here to fix the system, ma'am.

NUN 4   Call me Sister.

Scene Two: Gnostic Nuns at Terminals (GNAT): "From one word proceeds all things."

NUN 9   From one word proceeds all things.

NUN 3   Wonder

NUN 4   Underwood

NUN 2   Would you wonder

NUN 10   Underwood

NUN 5   The One

PRINT   Manual

NUN 6   Manual

INGRID   Seed

NUN 6   Under it all a read-only seed

NUN 1   F13

NUN 8   Stop

NUN 10   Enter

NUN 2   Sister

NUN 7   Sister

NUN 6   Sister

INGRID   They are —

WILKIE   The nuns in the ruins of this old convent —

NUNS   Old.

INGRID   When wonder of wonders it was in its days —

WILKIE   Alive in its days —

NUN 9   Print.

PRINT   Yes.

NUN 9   Problems. With the port.

PRINT   No, that's —

INGRID   They made their fortune.

NUN 1   Ceding fortune

NUN 2   Receding

NUN 5   I could tell you all about created things.

INGRID   Transcribing or enacting —

WILKIE   The works of Thomas à Kempis onto —

NUN 4   On the Internet.

INGRID   Limning or lighting up the —

NUN 3   To every other possible code

NUN 1   *The Imitation of Christ*

NUN 2   By Thomas à Kempis

INGRID   Imitated into every variety of code.

NUN 10   Center.

NUN 8   Sister?

NUN 9   Print.

PRINT   Yes?

NUN 9   You can see we're having problems with the —

PRINT   No. That's my name. Print.

NUNS
  Whirr
  Whirr
  Whirr
  From
  Friend
  Under
  Wonder
  Wonder
  O for a manual typewriter
  Old Underwood
  Wonderful Under
  Woulda Coulda
  Old
  Will you help us
  Print
  One Word?

BELLS   Strange and beautiful to see. To see strange and. Beautiful to see. Strange and beautiful.

Scene Three: Garden

ROBIN   Sister, I'll take you into the garden. We'll have breakfast there.

NUN 2   Late in the day.

WILKIE   Print traces back wires with a manual in his hand.

NUN 7   Manual typewriter.

NUN 6   Excuse me, what — ?

PRINT   This is like a Geiger counter. It reads the wires.

INGRID   The Bells are dressed like bells in a belfry.

BELLS   It's already late in the day.

PRINT   It's giving me Nathaniel Hawthorne.

WILKIE   The Bells read from Hawthorne's *Wonder Book for Boys and Girls*:

BELLS   "The old couple lived in their palace a great, great while, and grew older and older, and very old indeed. At length, however, there came a summer morning when Philemon and Baucis failed to make their appearance, as on other mornings, with one hospitable smile overspreading both their pleasant faces, to invite guests of overnight to breakfast."

NUN 8   It's the Bells. Bells!

ROBIN   Old sister sister Sister Milan, come out take your meal here by the Spanish lavender. Old sister sister Sister Milan come take your nourishment out by —

MILAN   The well and the flat stones for grinding and the tree and the tree's ladder and the wall.

BELLS   "The guests searched everywhere, from top to bottom of the spacious palace, and all to no purpose. Only after much perplexity did they espy in front of the patch two venerable trees which nobody could remember to have seen the day before. Yet there they stood, with their roots fastened deep into the soil, and a huge breadth of foliage over-shadowing the whole front of the edifice."

ROBIN   Get close.

NUN 1   Emperor birds.

NUN 7   Engaged.

NUN 1   Emperor birds in the nodes of future roots. Serve at the pleasure.

NUN 7   Sensing tremble by tap root, through to historical present.

NUN 1   Looking—

ROBIN   Here.

NUN 8   Sh.

ROBIN   Sister sit.

WILKIE   She cuts bell chords. The Bells still sing.

BELLS   "One was an oak and one was a linden. Their boughs—strange and beautiful to see—were intertwined, so that each tree seemed to live in the other tree's bosom more than in its own."
("One was an oak and one was a linden. Their boughs—strange and beautiful to see—were intertwined, so that each tree seemed to live in the other tree's bosom more than in its own.")

INGRID   Dryness flows from the blonde grass through the well's mud to the well.

NUN 6   Arriving at the junction box.

ROBIN, PRINT   Here we are.

NUN 8   Abbess climbs and puts her finger to the iron lip and the Hawthorne stops.

Scene Four: GNAT: "Keep silence."

NUN 10   Let

NUN 5   All

NUN 3   Teachers

NUN 2   Keep

NUN 8   Silence.

WILKIE   Captures the last Bell breaths in a box.

NUN 9   The nuns run submarine —

INGRID   Performing their functions with tongues and noses —

NUN 8   Hush for the Abbess.

NUN 1   Until they can get away with fingers again.

NUN 10   Let

NUN 7   All

NUN 5   Teachers —

WILKIE   She releases Bell breath into the garden.

NUN 4   Animates the insects and breath.

NUN 2   Robin feeds sweet in blur and dying Bells.

NUN 10   Keep

NUN 8   Silence.

Scene Five: Auto-Feed

INGRID   Tech support serpents through up from out of down to tech hidey hole.

NUN 3   Hello.

NUN 4   Hello.

NUN 6   Hello, Print.

PRINT   Try it now.

BELLS   Wipe.

WILKIE   The fading Bells repeat from the face of the abbess' index.

NUN 2   Feed.

NUN 10   Manual.

NUN 5   Feed.

BELLS   Wipe.

WILKIE   The bone in the Abbess's index rings where she touched the Bells.

NUN 2   Robin feeds her wipes her mouth Milan —

NUN 3, ROBIN   Lives off honey thinned with brandy.

INGRID   Carmelite brandy the mute nuns the liquor they —

NUN 4   We ferment behind closed lips.

WILKIE   Silence drunk.

INGRID   Thinning honey.

ROBIN   And dropped.

NUN 4   Thinned with whiskey.

ROBIN   Thinned with kiss.

INGRID   Sister Milan is the oldest sister in the place.

WILKIE   Feeds at an eyedropper loaded with fermented blackberry and honey.

ROBIN   I sit with her.

INGRID   Sister Robin is the youngest sister in the place.

MILAN   Sits with me.

NUN 3   Past the bean poles on a stone bench in the middle of beaten blonde weeds under a summer.

NUN 4   And a pear tree with old age mind disease hands off pears as misremembered images.

BELLS   Wipe.

NUN 8   Wind in the space between the Abbess and the Bells winds around the flow of iron and passes back hum.

NUN 1   In the future, for the children, it is night, though today shines through and makes night pale then.

MILAN   The youngest in the place —

NUN 7   The memories of the garden nuns, unbeknownst, are whispering out loud in the future, between the passing fingers of the beer tree.

MILAN   — In the place, takes care of me as a discipline against her falling asleep at prayers, four in the morning.

INGRID   Wide awake at fall.

BIRDS   She will be wide awake when she falls.

MILAN   Dropping pitchers and dishes, missing ingredients in the day's bake. The others don't realize that she's 'lept, narcolept, leapt out of herself and nympholept, fairy stolen. She —

ROBIN   Swoons —

MILAN   Against my last-rib breasts. O dear.

WILKIE   Milan marionettes Milan's —

NUN 4   Arms up to squeeze the alcoholic sweet out of the sticky dropper in between the lips of the —

NUNS 4, 9, 10   Sixteen-year-old.

WILKIE   Milan has the face of a window-killed bird.

INGRID   Robin has the throat and supple of a fawn.

NUN 3   Milan —

NUN 4   Works the liquor down the blue throat.

WILKIE   They allow Milan —

NUN 3   In a kind of creel —

WILKIE   The burned crusts of failed fruitcakes. She —

MILAN   I feed her these. Work her smooth jaw. Her lips part for chew.

Scene Six: GNAT: "We are exiles here."

NUN 5   We are exiles here.

NUN 8   We can put our trust in nothing in this world.

NUN 9   A man should place such complete trust in God —

NUN 5   That he has no need of comfort from men.

NUN 7   We transcend mere reason on the wings of a burning love for Him.

NUN 1   We transcend mere reason on the wings of a burning love for Him.

NUN 10   We transcend mere reason on the wings of a burning love for Him.

NUN 3   We transcend mere reason on the wings of a burning love for hum.

NUN 6   We transcend mere reason on the wings of a burning love for hum.

NUN 9   We transcend

NUN 8
> mere reason on

NUN 4
> the wings

NUN 5
> of a burning

NUNS   Love for Him.

NUN 4   Sadly, I am illiterate, and the others don't know.

BAT   How do you type?

NUN 4   Match shape for shape.

NUN 6   Type.

NUN 8   Type.

NUN 3   Type.

NUN 6   He moves through the nerves silver nerves as light through a spider web stretched in the goldenrod on the way to the pond by the powerlines.

WILKIE   Sight bends around event. Milan sees him bend past abbess, sees the repairman's crack and in abyss reflects.

MILAN   Pond by the powerlines.

NUN 3   Skinny dipping with the carpenter Roger Bardwell.

MILAN   Naked ten minutes.

NUN 3   Shining webs in dawn goldenrod.

WILKIE   Before she went to the bank and pulled the black habit from the tree and he —

MILAN   Discovered I was a nun.

PRINT   Tuck.

NUN 10   Whoever loves much, does much.

NUN 5   Whoever does a thing well, does much.

NUN 6   Do you like Print?

NUN 8   O Print's charming.

Scene Seven: Bardwell Skinny

NUNS   Drop on the trembling web.

NUN 9   What are you doing?

PRINT   Let me use your station.

NUNS   Downflow stream spinning web.

NUN 9   Why?

PRINT   I'm running a diagnostic.

INGRID   Powerlines, dropping current through cattle, boulevard through woods. Electricity sings with spiders.

WILKIE   Sister silver, sister bath.

NUN 6   Bardwell out of his truck.

NUN 3   The past. Her mind.

NUN 5   Wake up!

NUN 1   Wake up!

MILAN   Before Christ.

NUNS 3, 7, 10   Sixteen.

NUN 4   Pause, then feet on gravel; electricity hushes.

NUN 3   Truck; they vest.

MILAN   And the roof is left unmended.

INGRID/WILKIE   The birds sing —

BIRDS   Milan is remembering. Bardwell was hired to fix the roof.

MILAN, BIRDS   And he left; roof unmended.

NUN 5   In nuns' present:

NUN 4   Bats!

BELLS   Bats flow in through thatch when —

NUN 6   Print our imp.

NUN 4   Dot matrix, bats in flight, clears all, negative against positive print screen —

PRINT   Clear all.

NUN 10   Further further.

NUN 9   Scroll.

NUN 10   Further.

NUN 8   Further.

NUN 5   Further in dot matrix is —

NUN 4   Bats!

PRINT   You can go.

INGRID   Bat wing gust cleans dew from web.

NUN 9   It happens again and again.

WILKIE   They thought they were working against distraction. No.
They enter lives centered on distraction.

PRINT   Scroll. Scroll we go.

PRINT, BATS   Scroll scroll scroll we go/Gently down the
screen/Merrily merrily merrily merrily /
Strike through F13

Scene Eight: GNAT: "No city."

NUN 9   Here you have no abiding city

NUNS

Here you have no abiding city
Here you have no abiding city
Roan eats oats where bricks are grown
Shoat moans bones through ancient Rome
Hay breaks day

NUN 5   Here you have no abiding city.

Scene Nine: Snare

NUN 8   Sh.

ALL   Sh.

WILKIE   The nuns are asleep.

INGRID   Not all of them.

BELLS   The nuns are asleep or eyeballs are painted on their lids, punched loaves; heat low to the ground, cat in earthquake, earth-heat flatbelly and panicked under advancing; attached to and fearing beat; its only security, that which it fears.

INGRID   When it's still, everything's heart.

WILKIE   Print takes a snare brush and gently grazes sleepers here and there.

BATS   Sits at a station, turns a terminal up, and plays snare drum.

WILKIE   Nuns wake to *love* code, and encode faster.

INGRID   Robin and Milan are reborn out of thermal cat.

WILKIE   With new love.

INGRID   Wake and face each other in code and love.

Scene Ten: GNAT: "Spouse."

NUN 1:   Pum

NUN 7   Pup

NUNS 3, 9   Pum.

NUNS 3, 5, 7, 10   Toot the horn and bang the drum.

NUNS   The spouse the spouse has come has come.

NUNS 4, 5, 10   Soul, heart and time's curved event

BELLS   Ring!

NUNS 1, 3, 5, 10   Clapper, hollow and shape

NUNS   Ring!

NUN 4   Come then, faithful soul

NUNS 2, 6, 7, 10   Prepare your heart for your

NUNS   Divine spouse!

Scene Eleven: Honeyface (bats = bees)

INGRID   Reviving.

ROBIN   Sister sister sister I —

MILAN   That's okay.

WILKIE   So drunk they do not feel the bees sting their foreheads lips and windpipes.

INGRID   The bees are drunk on their brown blood.

BELLS   Wipe.

NUN 2   A bee changes direction, fights a bat for sugar. Robin —

INGRID   Levels her head, shakes.

(Thomas à Kempis)   173

ROBIN   Let's start.

NUN 2   She reveals to the bees: fat lips:

ROBIN   Cistern. Spigot dumps water from tapped spring into stone cistern whose overflow makes a waste stream through a low grated arch in the two-foot-thick outer walls. We wash sister out on the bench because:

NUN 3   More waste from her.

WILKIE   And the sun saves her life in the summer.

ROBIN   Soak —

INGRID   A clean rag.

MILAN   Scrap of virgin cheesecloth used to wrap the fruitcakes.

ROBIN   Balled in hand, revealed in trough, balled again, and I —

MILAN   Lean —

ROBIN   Sister against me backwards. Sister, you're old.

BELLS *(Repeating)*   Now.

ROBIN   You're growing a beard.

WILKIE   The softest hair she has is moss-soft by her lips and from her chin.

ROBIN   Drop the weight of my shoulder into her and lick a bead of liquor-cured honey from the hairs at the corner of her mouth.

NUN 3   Milan. Her throat swells.

WILKIE   Bee-victim.

MILAN   Well here we are.

INGRID   Between bells.

ROBIN   I may remove her wimple, and do. Mine too. They don't know
I let the hair of her head grow long, gray hair long —

NUN 3   Creepers with mind-in-sap.

ROBIN   I shrug out shoulder and lay her hair across me where my
cropped hair won't go.

NUN 2   Robin was left, a loaf.

NUN 9   At our doorstep.

NUN 4   Doorstep.

NUN 7, INGRID   Doorstep baby.

Scene Twelve: GNAT: "Purity enjoys . . ."

NUN 4   Simplicity

NUN 7   Reaches

NUN 8   Out

NUN 1   After

NUN 5   God.

NUN 9   Purity

NUN 6   Discovers

NUN 10   And enjoys

NUN 8   Him.

NUN 10   Simplicity reaches out after God. Purity discovers and enjoys him.

NUN 9   Purity:

NUN 10   The lake is what it is

NUN 5   Reflecting.

Scene Thirteen: Swallow through Barn

BELLS   Swallow.

ROBIN   I'm wide awake.

NUNS   Swallow.

INGRID   Sister Robin rights Sister Milan and flies over the steno pool.

NUNS 3, 4, 7   Swallow through the barn.

NUNS 1, 2, 6, 8   Swallow through the barn.

ROBIN   It's been five minutes and it's been ten minutes. Now we go outside and play.

NUN 2   Robin fetches her galoshes.

NUN 8   Swallow through the barn.

BELLS, NUN 9   Swallow.

PRINT   Wait and stay and —

WILKIE   Doses Milan with another nitro.

ROBIN   I'm wide awake. What do we play now?

Scene Fourteen: GNAT: "Regard as empty."

NUNS 1, 2, 6, 8   Regard as empty comfort all things that derive from creatures.

NUNS 3, 4, 7   Regard as empty comfort all things that derive from creatures.

NUN 5   Regard as empty

NUN 9   Comfort all things

NUN 4   That

NUN 10   Derive from creatures.

NUNS 2, 3   Regard empty

NUNS 1, 7   All

NUNS 1, 6, 8   All things derive from creature comforts regard

NUNS 1, 3, 4, 5, 10   Empty

NUN 4   That

BELLS   Swallow.

Scene Fifteen: Pear tree. Ladder. Wall. Tower.

MILAN   Where are you doing?

ROBIN   Going.

MILAN   Where?

INGRID   She goes juvie!

ROBIN   Over the wall.

NUN 2   Over the wall.

INGRID   Takes an apron full of pears.

ROBIN   Tosses them down.

NUN 2   Takes ladder.

ROBIN   Take.

INGRID   To the wall.

NUN 2   And up and over.

ROBIN   You can eat. Show me.

NUN 4   Drip and maceration.

INGRID   Seems to swallow them whole herself.

ROBIN   Up and over.

WILKIE   Climbs over the wall?

ROBIN   Yes, sister, do.

NUN 4   No food then sudden food dizzy, plus the honeydrunk —

WILKIE   Robin climbs first, Milan follows. Robin passes the ladder over, climbs down first.

NUN 8   False liberty of mind.

ROBIN   Here.

MILAN   What now?

ROBIN   What do you want to play? We have a picnic. Let's play . . .

MILAN   What. A game where I don't move.

ROBIN   I'll show you a trick we can do.

INGRID   And she lays the ladder against a wooden phone pole, over which the high intensity wires are draped.

BELLS   Swallow.

INGRID   When she ran through the pool she ran to get her stick.

PRINT   This is a simple story. Two girls from the future dream about the dawn of the twenty-first century while drinking beer from the beer tree that overlooks the ruin of an old convent. They imagine the nuns imputing Thomas à Kempis' *Imitation of Christ*, translating it into various languages, adapting it to different genres . . .

NUN 6 *(Revealing/sharing the secret)*   The girls from the future imagine the oldest and the youngest nun, out of bounds, looking after each other. The youngest wants to prove she can touch a high intensity wire with a stick and not get shocked.

PRINT   Don't look. They die.

NUN 2   No. Show it again. This time give her the —

INGRID   Lickety-split, smashes glass, gets the important stick.

WILKIE   Climbs to show that because her boots are rubber —

NUN 9   The youth.

NUN 2   And because she is not touching the wire.

INGRID   In her impatience.

ROBIN   But the *stick* is —

INGRID   She can do her one thing.

WILKIE   She can touch the wire in a way and not be hurt.

NUN 2   Girl climbs aluminum in the morning and reaches for the wire.

NUN 9, MILAN   Youth up in day. Aluminum.

INGRID   Her luck —

Scene Sixteen: GNAT: "The holy spirit comes and goes."

WILKIE   A flock of ill-assorted doves come.

NUNS 2, 7   Pear tree. Ladder. Wall. Tower.

NUNS 4, 6, 8   Arc and fall.

NUNS 9, 10   The Holy Spirit comes and goes.

NUNS 1, 3, 5, 9, 10
    Wrens wrench the finch winch
    Runaway parrot chain slips again
    Something absurd about those hummingbirds

Massing assassin with the berrybush thrushes
Fools rush in

INGRID   Print scrapes a snare brush along live conduit and firefly the
bats revive so —

NUN 10   The war between the bats and birds.

NUN 8   Bat against dove. Wings of one form throat of other.

NUN 5   Positive negative locked in on and on.

NUN 9   How the Holy Spirit would love to be assumed by the color behind, day when it's day, night when it's night, it sometimes matches.

Scene Seventeen: Arc and Fall

ROBIN   Watch me.

MILAN   Get down from there.

ROBIN   Watch —

MILAN   Hey, kid, get down from there —

ROBIN   What I can do.

MILAN   This instant.

NUN 2   She climbs up the utility pole.

PRINT   Their minds are clearing.

ROBIN   I have a theory.

MILAN   I want you to come down. How's that for a theory?

ROBIN   I can show you a game.

WILKIE   She says it's dangerous.

INGRID   She says it's fine.

NUN 1   Birds watch her climb to the wire.

NUN 7   With her stick in her hand and rubber shoes —

ROBIN   On my feet.

MILAN   Come here again and again the garden the heat I want to sit
with you in the garden again and again on a usual day it is my training
these many years.

ROBIN   I can touch the wire and not feel it if I touch with a stick and
wear rubber galoshes.

MILAN   Whyever would you want to?

ROBIN   To show you one thing once today old woman because I like
you now watch.

WILKIE   These:

INGRID   These you count with birds of different genus or one hand.

BIRDS, BELLS   One.

NUN 2   Baby sister falls asleep at the top of the pole, one arm locked
around, and the other arm out with the stick. Falls asleep. A stick.

BIRDS, BELLS   Two.

WILKIE   The stick taps the wire.

BIRDS, BELLS   Three.

NUN 2   The spirits —

NUN 5   Ill assorted birds —

NUN 2   Fly up. The wire swings, and tap tap the Morse code stick.

BIRDS, BELLS   Four.

NUN 3   The bearded woman sees her young charge jammed against the sign when the arc strikes.

INGRID   For even though there is no direct contact, the instant-girl, so happy, between heaven and earth, is placed where the flow of rampaging code can jump.

WILKIE   Jump in and reach from flow to moment in her.

NUNS 1, 2, 3, 7   Arc.

INGRID, WILKIE   And fall.

INGRID   Five. Fall.

WILKIE   She drops right on to the poor old woman.

NUNS 2, 3   Two hearts attacked.

BELLS
Once
Once upon
Once upon a time
Once upon a time

INGRID   Young sister has a heart attack and dies on the instant. Old sister has a heart attack and waits, because she has had them before.

Waits 'til she forgets all that. The moment of spark and the size of Robin's fall and her attack and final thought never change, have no possibilities, but continue to happen.

WILKIE   As witnessed by us —

INGRID   And related —

WILKIE   At the pleasure of the Empire.

INGRID   Pass a fruit please.

INGRID, WILKIE   Hello Sister Milan. Hello.

Scene Eighteen: GNAT: "Born to work."

NUN 9   Why do you look for rest —

NUNS   Since you are born to work?

PRINT   Overload and —

Scene Nineteen: System Crash

PRINT   System crash.

MILAN   Lights out.

NUN 3   Hello? Hello Sister are you there?

NUN 6   Are you there?

NUN 4   Thought I saw —

NUN 9   What?

NUN 8   What.

NUN 7   Did you see any —

NUN 1   No.

NUN 10   We've crashed.

NUN 9   Use the flares.

NUN 5   I've got a sodium light on batteries.

NUN 4   Eat peppermints.

NUN 8   The shades aren't drawn, you know.

NUNS 2, 3   Oh.

NUNS 1, 7   My eyes haven't adjusted.

NUNS 4, 5, 6, 8   We —

NUNS 5, 9, 10   Crashed.

PRINT   I can run a patch.

NUN 10   Do we lose data?

PRINT   Watch your screens. Don't look at me. Watch!

NUNS   Ahh.

INGRID   They pick up.

MILAN   Robin, can you move?

WILKIE   They pick up. Incident, unread.

MILAN   Robin?

INGRID   Where they left.

NUNS   Ahh.

WILKIE   Light on their faces. Lowering sun on fulcrum over hills, lifts dark up over their knees and desks, lifts light away.

Scene Twenty: GNAT: "Master."

NUN 9   Pleased.

NUN 1   Conqueror of self

NUN 2   Master of the world

NUN 3   Around the moment, hell's wealth is pearled.

NUN 4   Pearls in a row

NUN 5   Helled to necklace

NUN 6   Basic black

NUN 7   Hell's bells

NUN 8   Time and place

NUN 10   Heart attack

BELLS
  Conqueror of self
  Master of the world.

WILKIE   They'll do better.

INGRID   They'll do better.

BELLS
They'll do better, in the future
They'll do better, in the future

Scene Twenty-One: Pear Pair

ROBIN   Because of the seeds we carry inside from our eating this morning, and because, first cause, the us that carries them, when I die and I am
dead with you we grow to be new creatures by the pond and the utility
poles.

NUN 7   Stop. I can hear the trees grow. Resume.

MILAN   With you not to feed me and me not to you in the hurt of the
full sun same as dark with croak-eyed adjust; with me cleaned for death
and you be-stinked for death . . . our two coherencies break to sighs, give
up ghosts; pick up sticks. I turn into a tree and take you with me. My
gray hair rises to branches. The yellow nails on my bare feet spade out
holes. I put my arms around you and take you to tree. To one. Up higher.
Intersapping, past exchange, sequence, return. One. Tree of the future.
Whisper. Up. Our habits break and the skin blisters to bark. Where we
are absolute twin at twists and groans, the old woman squeal at wind,
rubbed branches leaking honey down arms . . . Christ to cross, old old
Jesus intervoluting with his young living cross; nails: topiary, training my
reach through you. You sprout feather-shaped leaves from hands made
of pure nerves, each nerve a separate finger tickling into my hands. Roots
down, gravity against, and skyward Eden-play, open heads, open
crowns, budding, not knowing. You see, this is what you get when you
love an old woman. This is what you get. We count each other's fingers —
the sum changing every time. The changing, whispered sum is Love. The
squeak of our rubbing in the wind is "I love you." The sun in our
branches is the station of our round secret. The other sisters find two
trees growing into one. Miracle!

NUN 1   The beer-fruit tree.

Scene Twenty-Two: GNAT: "Feast/Fasting."

NUN 6   Packing up?

PRINT   You're all together.

NUN 10   It will go much faster now.

ALL NUNS BUT 6   Same same same

NUNS 5, 7, 9   Faster, slower

NUNS 1, 2, 3, 8   In. Formation.

NUN 6   Thank you.

PRINT   Good-bye.

NUN 6   Linger.

NUN 8   Sh.

NUN 6   Linger. Won't you — could you — ? I can —

NUN 9   He finds many to share his feast, but few his fasting.

NUNS 1, 2, 3, 8   Faster, slower

NUNS 5, 7, 9   Same same same

NUNS   In. Formation.

Scene Twenty-Three: Starry Crown

BELLS   Years go by and the convent fails.

NUN 10   Logging off here.

NUN 5   Logging off.

BELLS   Trees break up through the floors, lance walls, corrupt square joints and the place is claimed by a forest of hybrids; unpicked fruit brews on the vines. It will be perfect then.

NUN 4   Logging off.

NUN 8   Logging off.

INGRID   The Bells fall against themselves at each new rearrangement.

NUN 6   Print is where he wants to be, where he wanted to be all along. Screensaver. Down in the viruses, down with the code. Alterman Print is working out pi without ever using it. Circle Milan uses/used point Robin to round. Hell around heaven, purgatory pi.

BELLS   Deeply entangled. Print eats cold wires in the cab of his truck. Print and Bats eat circle's secret.

NUN 6   The story of Robin and Milan stored by some of us as private virus in between Kempis code. Print purifies the system. So we have no was or will or will have been, strictly *ising* and this this this he tracks pures and makes all things happen and happen and happen. Line in a line.

NUN 1   Ingrid and Wilkie climb.

NUN 7   Eating all the beer pears they can find after the harvest.

INGRID   Slurping the juice —

NUN 6   Robin made it happen once and Milan knew it.

NUN 7   — Of the fruit, ripe or not.

NUN 1   Ingrid and Wilkie make it happen once again. Only and ever.

NUN 7   Once upon a time once once.

NUN 6   I do not believe the devil runs Hell. He runs purgatory. Hell and heaven are complete and need gods. Purgatory is labor and that that that, always happen, completing compleading please won't you help me print one —

NUN 9   Logging off here, and there.

NUN 6   Logging. Off.

INGRID   Burping, singing Weeblo songs with nasty lyrics.

NUN 7   Till they sing themselves into the limbs of the original twins.

ROBIN, MILAN   The thick of the original whisper.

INGRID   Wilkie wears special mittens to keep from scratching herself at night. They get secured with plastic ties her parents have to cut off in the mornings. Wilkie lets me put different colors of licorice in her mouth to see the colors they turn her tongue. Wilkie bites peppermints to show me how the sparks come. Wilkie is all the mouth for the two of us because I have a wrap-around retainer so she sometimes chews the fruit and kisses beer into me like passing Houdini a key through bars. Younger and faster, she is in a crux above me. I look up. I see stars. And stars bouncing off the brass buckle of the Cub Scout belt she took from her brother when he quit.

WILKIE   Out of beer but still wanting to change our eyes, we pull sight from stars in the whisper and shift. We reach, plus our laughing and the stars shocked quiver over/under betting on our laughter pull down to fill night's pail and night's pale ale. We move.

NUN 4   As Robin, too, awake at fall; but since all is one there is no drop; it's being in the same place in a different way!

MILAN   Ingrid and Wilkie, stars come straight out of their heads and enter the mind of the pond. Their thoughts —

NUN 4   At that very moment

BELLS   Add stars —

NUNS 1, 7   To stars.

MILAN   To the reflected stars, silly stars. The sky reflects —

NUNS   At that —

ROBIN   The pool's stars back, the tree is at center of heaven and picture of heaven. Emperor birds contemplate the tree and are not in it, are the rapture of the tree between perception and origin.

NUNS   At that very moment.

WILKIE   Milan and Robin at once in the science fiction comprehension of water laughing —

NUNS   Every imitation of Him.

INGRID   Whisper in intervals between ghost bells clapping.

BELLS
    Stars
    Are
    Start
    Sorry
    Ess
    So
    See
    Sring
    See
    See
    Sring
    Sing
    Ding
    Ding

Sing
Song
Ding
Song
Ding
Ding
Every imitation of Him is
One is
Him is
Every imitation of Him is Him
Is every
One is one is
Every song is imitation of Him
Is see
Sing ding
Dong ding ding ding.

SONG FOR THE END

Song for the End closed out the Intersection *Saint Plays* (Intersection for the Arts, San Francisco, April 1993, Paul Codiga, Artistic Director and producer).

Live Music: Edith Rules (Derek Cheever, Leslie Jackson, Alan Whitman). Singers: Edith Rules and Jennifer Bainbridge, Denise Cavaliere, Sammie Choy, Troy Anthony Harris, Robert Molossi, Johnna Marie Schmidt, and David Todd.

One night you argue until you're tired and you
Open the door and three birds fly away
As if they were speaking secrets about you
It's night and three birds fly away

And you hope the gossips understand your secrets
Birds flash red throats and thread through the sky
Where have you been that birds speak your secrets?
Will they understand later and elsewhere in the sky?

And this will never happen again
The birds have flown with your secrets to heaven
Where will you go where have you been?
And this will never happen again

Your reason is bird gossip
And the three birds have all flown
And the gossip breaks down to metered prayer
And the birds have become unreasonable angels
Singing back all you've ever known

And you stand at the door and watch
The night birds fly away with your secrets
And you turn back to the kitchen table with
New love in your heart

And you take your lover's hands
And you have no secrets
You are understood elsewhere you have no reason for reasons
The birds have told your secrets as light to the heavens

And this will never happen again
And this will never happen again
And this will never happen again
And this will never happen again
The end

Library of Congress Cataloging-in-Publication Data
Ehn, Erik.
The saint plays / Erik Ehn.
p. cm. — (PAJ books)
ISBN 0-8018-6287-6 (pbk. : alk. paper)
1. Christian saints — Drama.   2. Christian drama, American.
I. Title.   II. Series.
PS3555.H58 S25 2000
812'.54 — dc21   99-050722